"Intuition is a concept that, until now, hasn't taken its rightful place in the practical businessman's lexicon. But after Roy Rowan's book, no up-and-coming businessman will ignore this elusive factor. At least, that's my intuitive feeling."
—Howard Stein
Chairman and CEO, Dreyfus Corporation

"Mr. Rowan makes a compelling case for the old-fashioned hunch."
—*New York Times*

"Roy Rowan's *The Intuitive Manager* will make every CEO reconsider his attitude about the use of intuition in managing a company or corporation. It is a thought-provoking and informative book."
—Roger Staubach
Former star quarterback of Dallas Cowboys
President, The Staubach Company

"This is a fascinating book on a fascinating subject. Managers everywhere will learn a great deal about themselves and their business decisions from reading it."
—Mary Kay Ash
Founder and CEO, Mary Kay Cosmetics

MORE . . .

THE
INTUITIVE
MANAGER
ROY ROWAN

B

BERKLEY BOOKS, NEW YORK

This Berkley book contains the complete
text of the original hardcover edition.
It has been completely reset in a typeface designed
for easy reading and was printed from new film.

THE INTUITIVE MANAGER

A Berkley Book / published by arrangement with
Little, Brown and Company

PRINTING HISTORY
Little, Brown edition / April 1986
Berkley trade paperback edition / September 1987
Berkley mass market edition / December 1991

ISBN: 0-425-13079-7

A BERKLEY BOOK ® TM 757,375
Berkley Books are published by The Berkley Publishing Group,
200 Madison Avenue, New York, New York 10016.
The name "BERKLEY" and the "B" logo
are trademarks belonging to Berkley Publishing Corporation.

PRINTED IN THE UNITED STATES OF AMERICA

10 9 8 7 6 5 4 3 2 1

For Helen, *my* intuitive manager

CONTENTS

ACKNOWLEDGMENTS

THIS book is drawn mainly from interviews over the past few years with many captains of American companies, plus a few men and women who have recently relinquished the helm. Several other leaders from the halls of academia and science also contributed valuable thoughts. I would particularly like to thank for their help and cooperation:

William Agee, former chairman, Bendix Corporation; Professor Weston Agor, University of Texas, El Paso; Mary Kay Ash, CEO, Mary Kay Cosmetics; Ralph Bahna. president, Cunard Line; John F. Bergin, president, McCann-Erickson U.S.A.; Robert Bernstein, chairman, Random House; Senator Bill Bradley; John Brodie, former San Francisco 49ers quarterback and now NBC sportscaster; Edgar Bronfman, chairman, Joseph E. Seagram & Sons; Helen Gurley Brown, editor, *Cosmopolitan*; aerobics specialist Dr. Kenneth Cooper; Rance Crain, president, Crain Communications; Frank Crerie, chairman, Stan West Mining Corporation; developer Trammell Crow; Willie Davis, former defensive captain, Green Bay Packers, now president, All-Pro Broadcasting; Professor Robert Doktor, University of Hawaii; author Peter Drucker; Billy Joe DuPree, former Dallas Cowboys tight end, now president, DuPree Construction Company; Solomon Dutka, CEO, Audits & Surveys Inc.; Richard Farson, president, Western Behavioral Sciences Institute; John Fetzer, chairman, Fetzer Broadcasting Company and Detroit Tigers; Debbi Fields, president, Mrs. Fields Cookies; book publisher Eleanor Friede; the late architect and engineer R. Buckminster

Fuller; Dr. Eugene Gendlin, University of Chicago; J. Peter Grace, chairman, W.R. Grace & Company; Bruce Gray, president, R.R. Bowker; Robert Greber, president, Lucasfilm Ltd.; Alyce Green, Menninger Foundation; Steven Greenberg, chairman, Anametrics Inc.; Armand Hammer, chairman, Occidental Petroleum; pollster Louis Harris; Christie Ann Hefner, president, Playboy Enterprises; Ned Herrmann, chairman, Whole Brain Corporation; Charles Hess, Inferential Focus; Matina Horner, president, Radcliffe College; executive search specialist E. Pendleton James, former White House personnel director; Professor Eugene Jennings, Michigan State University; Robert P. Jensen, chairman, E.F. Hutton LBO Inc.; Dr. E. Roy John, director of brain research, New York University Medical Center; Herman Kahn, deceased director, Hudson Institute; Rosabeth Moss Kanter, chairman, Goodmeasure Inc., and professor, Yale School of Management; Ray Kroc, deceased developer and chairman, McDonald's fast-food chain; movie producer Sherry Lansing, former president, Twentieth Century-Fox; Drew Lewis, former Secretary of Transportation, now chairman, Warner Amex Cable Communications; Stephen Lieber, president, Lieber & Company, and founder, Evergreen funds; Frank Lorenzo, chairman, Continental Airlines; management consultant Patricia Luciani; venture capitalist David Mahoney, former CEO, Norton Simon; William May, former chairman, American Can Company; Joseph McKinney, chairman, Tyler Corporation; Carl Menk, chairman, Cany, Bowen Inc.; Professor John Mihalasky, New Jersey Institute of Technology; Professor Henry Mintzberg, McGill University; former astronaut Edgar Mitchell, founder, Institute of Noetic Sciences; Dr. Paul Mok, president, Training Associates; venture capitalist Terry Opdendyk, partner, ONSET; David Packard, chairman, Hewlett-Packard; H. Ross Perot, chairman, Electronic Data Systems Corporation; Joseph Potts, executive director, National Training Laboratory; Nancy Reynolds, president, Wexler, Reynolds, Harrison & Schule; Russell Reynolds, Jr., chairman, Russell Reynolds Associates; developer James Rouse; Donald Rumsfeld, former Secretary of Defense, and recently resigned chairman, G.D. Searle; Patricia Ryan, managing editor, *Peo-*

ple; Dr. Jonas Salk, discoverer of the antipolio vaccine and founding director, Salk Institute for Biological Studies; Irving Shapiro, former chairman, Du Pont, presently a law partner at Skadden Arps Slate Meagher & Flom; Frederick Smith, chairman, Federal Express; Roger Staubach, former Dallas Cowboys quarterback, now president, Staubach Company; Howard Stein, chairman, Dreyfus Corporation; Geraldine Stutz, president, Henri Bendel; Deborah Szekely, founder, Golden Door, presently president, Inter-American Foundation; Fran Tarkenton, former Minnesota Vikings quarterback, now chairman, Tarkenton Productivity Group; John Teets, chairman, Greyhound Corporation; fashion designer Diane Von Furstenberg; Thomas Wyman, chairman, CBS Inc.; and Professor Abraham Zaleznik, Harvard Business School.

I am also grateful to Genevieve Young, my friend and editor at Little, Brown, who straightened out a few twists and turns in this tour of intuition, and who helped make a slippery road a little easier for readers to travel.

Most of all, I am indebted to Time Inc. for dispatching me all over the world during the past thirty-eight years, first in the pursuit of stories for *Life*, then for *Time*, and finally for *Fortune*—a fascinating journey on which I encountered most of the people who appear on the following pages.

in·tu·i·tion (ĭn´ tû·ĭsh´ ŭn), *n.* [ML. *intuitio*, fr. L. *intuori* to look on, fr. *in-* in, on + *tuerï. See TUITION.*] **1.** *Obs.* a A looking upon; a seeing either with the physical eye or with the "eye of the mind"; contemplation; sight. b An indirect or ulterior view; regard; reference.
2. Knowledge obtained, or the power of knowing, without recourse to inference or reasoning; innate or instinctive knowledge; insight; familiarly, a quick or ready insight or apprehension. "Sagacity and a nameless something more,— let us call it *intuition.*" *Hawthorne.*
3. *Philos.* Immediate apprehension or cognition; either the faculty or power of such apprehension or a particular act or instance of it. *Intuition* is applied to direct or immediate knowing, whether mystical, perceptional, intellectual, or moral; and is, in general, contrasted with speculative, reflective, or mediate knowing.

—*Webster's New International
Dictionary of the
English Language*

THE
INTUITIVE
MANAGER

I

THE EUREKA FACTOR

1

WHAT IT IS

"HUNCH" is an odious word to the professional manager. It's a horseplayer's or stock market plunger's term, rife with imprecision and unpredictability. Yet, even in today's empirical world of business, where the fast track is paved over with MBAs who can figure the risk-reward ratio of any decision at the drop of a computer key, the old-fashioned hunch continues to be an important, though unappreciated, managerial tool. Logic and analysis can lead a person only partway down the path to a profitable decision. The last step to success frequently requires a daring intuitive leap, as many chief executives who control the destinies of America's biggest corporations will reluctantly concede.

Just as often the biggest roadblock to creative decision-making is not having the guts to follow a good hunch. And in no place is that roadblock more inhibiting than the boardroom. "The chief executive officer is not supposed to say, 'I feel.' He's supposed to say, 'I know,'" says David Mahoney, former chairman of Norton Simon and now head of his own venture capital company in New York City. Mahoney is one of those executives who secretly prize their business intuition. But since management is an inexact science, frequently defined as the art of making decisions with insufficient information, even the most deliberate boss is sometimes forced to act prematurely on nebulous inner impressions.

Nevertheless, it's hard for a manager to heed those nagging voices from some mysterious echo chamber deep inside his brain without sounding very unprofessional. Like Mahoney, any self-respecting chief executive is loath to admit that an important decision is based on an ill-defined gut feeling. "So we deify the word 'instinct' by calling it 'judgment,'" he says.

Yet, psychologists contend, feelings need no reasons. They know that a person doesn't pull answers out of a void, that intuition operates on subterranean levels where information is not consciously available. Although the realization may arrive at a seemingly magical moment, it comes usually after a long, hard pondering of a problem.

Archimedes, the ancient Greek physicist, was taking a bath, mulling over a question posed by King Hiero II of Syracuse—whether the king's crown was made of pure gold or alloyed with silver—when a way of finding the answer hit him. Observing the overflow from his tub, Archimedes realized that since gold is more dense than silver, a given weight of the yellow metal would displace less water. Excited by his discovery, he streaked out of his home without his clothes, shouting, "Eureka!" ("I have found it"). Archimedes then demonstrated to the king that his crown displaced more water than an equal weight of pure gold, proving that it was indeed fashioned from an alloy.

The Eureka factor, that sudden, illuminating "I've found it" flash, has been referred to again and again by scientists attempting to describe the key element in their discovery process. Most are quick to admit that scientific break-throughs do not seem to evolve slowly from a sequence of deductions. They spring finally from hunches that cannot be completely explained. "There are no logical paths to these [natural] laws," admitted Albert Einstein. "Only intuition resting on sympathetic understanding of experience can reach them." He called the theory of relativity "the happiest thought of my life."

Artists, certainly, have always assumed that creativity doesn't spring from a deductive assault on a problem. Yet there are instances where a melding of the intuitive and deductive helped produce magnificent results. From Leonardo da Vinci's pen flowed detailed drawings of the first flying machine, while much more recently from sculptor Ladislas Biro's imagination emerged the ballpoint pen. Both Robert Fulton, inventor of the steamboat, and Samuel Morse, inventor of the telegraph, started out life as artists. But intuition led them elsewhere.

Athletes, too, continue to demonstrate uncanny intuitive abilities. John Brodie, former quarterback of the San Francisco 49ers, refers to the "extraordinary state of mind" that performing sports stars sometimes get into, giving them a heightened focus and perception. Basketball star Larry Bird of the Boston Celtics says: "It's scary. When I'm at my best I can do just about anything I want and no one can stop me. I feel like I'm in total control of everything." Sometimes after shooting he'll turn tail and recoil down the court elated even before the ball has reached the basket. "I already know it's all net," he says.

Politics, we know, rewards its intuitive practitioners and demolishes those who can't sniff the winds correctly. Successful politicians have the ability to nudge public thinking positively or negatively, conservatively or innovatively, as long as they are within what John F. Kennedy called "the jaws of consent." The President told veteran pollster Lou Harris that most of the time he had confidence in his gut feelings. "But the time to scramble and take a poll," he warned, "is when you sense that you have made a decision that may be outside the jaws of consent."

A master of political timing, Ronald Reagan innately senses whenever those jaws are about to snap shut. That son of Eureka (Illinois) College has tried to beguile America into believing he is just an actor, while actually he is one of the most intuitive politicians ever to occupy the White House—and one of the Eureka factor's best salesmen. "The amazing thing," says Harris, "is how unerring his instinct is in knowing when to duck, when to go for the jugular, and how to go for broke communicating about it. He is the absolute opposite of Jimmy Carter, who immersed himself in detail and never sensed his political options."

John Sears, Reagan's former campaign adviser, pointed out right after the 1984 election: "Reagan has given us one thing the people will cling to regardless of our future problems. He has presided over the restoration of our confidence. Blindly optimistic, fiercely patriotic, and unbending in his loyalty, he is the embodiment of a peculiar American virtue that says that all things are possible if you will just make them so—that reality is an illusion that can be overcome."

It is the corporate leader, usually an appointee of the board of directors, who needs a little prompting on the powers of intuition. Once the modern manager understands how intuition works, he or she (after all, it is said to be "woman's intuition") may not be afraid to recognize that "a funny feeling" on the way to a decision can be crucial and worth paying attention to.

And it isn't just the big boss who needs this reassurance. Every employee makes decisions, if only what course of action to recommend to the bird one branch higher in the corporate pecking order. As a manager is promoted, the farther into the unpredictable future his decisions reach and the more he must rely on intuition. "Things keep changing too frequently, so planning may do more damage than good," says Howard Stein, who started out to be a concert violinist and is now chairman of the Dreyfus Corporation, which manages some forty mutual funds. "By the time you get a program approved, and people are committed to it, things change and it doesn't work." His prescription for using intuition is: "Make a decision, move forward, but don't feel wedded to what you're doing."

Male or female, top brass or lowly trainee, the decision-maker needs to understand how the brain constantly delves into the subconscious to retrieve buried fragments of knowledge and experience, which it then instantaneously fuses with new information. Appreciating the biological basis of this retrieval system may not make it easier to define a hunch or defend its reliability. But understanding how intuition works should make it seem less necessary to cover one's intuitive tracks or to offer some lame excuse to conceal the importance of intuition in arriving at a decision.

A HERITAGE OF PROFITABLE HUNCHES

The intuitive boss, after all, is a recurring figure in American business. Cornelius Vanderbilt consulted clairvoyants and believed in ghosts, J. P. Morgan was known to visit fortune-tellers, while H. L. Hunt relied on a psychic to help pick oil properties. Traditionally, American entrepreneurs have taken enormous pride in their enormously profitable hunches, though usually without the counsel of mediums.

When Ray Kroc, the late hamburger king, was a boy his father took him to a phrenologist. "I was told that I would make my best living either in the food business or as a musician," he recalled. And he did both. After serving in the Red Cross Ambulance Corps in World War I, Kroc played piano in Chicago bars and restaurants and sold paper cups. His keyboard ability never earned him much of a living, but he sold enough cups to become midwest sales manager for Lily-Tulip. In 1937 he quit to buy exclusive sales rights to the "multimixer," a machine that could whip up six milkshakes at once.

In 1952 Richard and Maurice McDonald ordered eight multimixers for one restaurant in San Bernardino, California, pricking Kroc's curiosity about what kind of place could generate such a big order. So he flew out to deliver the multimixers himself. "When I got there," said Kroc, "I saw more people waiting in line than I had ever seen at any drive-in. I said to myself, 'Son of a bitch, these guys have got something.'"

Kroc talked the brothers into letting him franchise their outlets nationwide. During the next five years he organized a chain of 228 McDonald's. But he was collecting less than 2 percent of the gross and had to turn over more than a quarter of that to the brothers. Frustrated, he called the brothers in 1960 and asked them to quote a price for everything, including the name. They did—$2.7 million— and they also pulled the original San Bernardino restaurant out of the deal. Advised by his lawyer not to pay the exorbitant price, Kroc recalled: "I'm not a gambler and I didn't have that kind of money, but my funnybone instinct kept urging me on. So I closed my office door, cussed up and down, and threw things out the window. Then I called my lawyer back and said: 'Take it!' "

John Teets, chairman of the Greyhound Corporation, who is pictured in his company's dramatic two-page magazine ads peering perceptively over the Grand Canyon and other great American vistas, says, "What appears as a highly intuitive move at the time it is being made usually seems like common sense in retrospect." Even the most daring business gambles, he claims, "look safe and sensible once they succeed." The investment banking community was extremely critical of his plans to restructure Greyhound. But the price of its stock doubled after he did.

In Teets's view, intuition is often augmented by adversity. At age thirty he was the father of two daughters and half-owner of a thriving restaurant, shopping center, and ice-skating complex in Meadowdale, Illinois. "Although I hadn't gone to college," he says, "I felt that I knew how to create things and make them work."

But that year a series of personal tragedies struck. His wife and brother died. Then the same week that President Kennedy was assassinated the "fireproof" steel-and-concrete complex burned to the ground in the biggest fire Meadowdale ever had. "Those bitter experiences taught me that some occurrences are totally out of our control," says Teets. "I was severely depressed. But I never lost hope. My intuition told me that things would somehow work out." While deciding whether or not to rebuild the burned-out complex, he was offered a job running Greyhound's restaurants at the 1964 New York World's Fair. He calls intuition an "inexplicable interior force that resides in a halfway house between egotism and humility."

The feisty founder and chairman of Electronic Data Systems Corporation, H. Ross Perot, followed his gut feelings through a series of career changes from Texarkana (Texas) Junior College, to the U.S. Naval Academy, to IBM, from which he broke away to start up the Dallas-based computer services giant, EDS. In 1984 he became one of the biggest stockholders of General Motors, when it acquired his company for $2.5 billion.

Perot recalls a study done at Annapolis to find out what instinct made some midshipmen better leaders than others. The answer, he says, "was an intuitive feeling of being able to win, though in nearly every case it was not known how." When two of his EDS employees were taken prisoner in Iran in 1978, Perot personally mounted a commando force to free them. He didn't know how their escape would be worked out, but instinctively he felt it would succeed, and remarkably it did.

And how does Perot describe intuition? "It means *knowing your business*," he says, drawling out the three words for emphasis. "It means being able to bring to bear on a situation everything you've seen, felt, tasted, and experienced in an industry." Perot claims he operates a memo-less company. Like Napoleon, who reputedly tossed out all written reports from his generals, figuring he'd already heard the important news, Perot prefers to conduct all of his business by personal contact. "Written reports stifle creativity," he says. "They discourage the reader from responding intuitively."

Hardly had GM acquired EDS when the giant automaker's innovative chief, Roger Smith, announced at a staff meeting that Perot had a new mission. He was to transform GM's Saturn project—which was charged not only with turning out a revolutionary new car, but a whole new production system—into a paperless company. Both men knew what a hard job this would be in a bureaucracy like GM. "Smith," said Perot, "looked over at me and winked. He knew he dropped a boulder on my shoulder."

One Sunday morning Eleanor Friede, then an editor with Macmillan and now an independent book producer, was sitting on the deck of her beach house in East Hampton, Long Island, reading a dog-eared manuscript for a children's book that had made the rounds of two dozen publishing houses without a single taker. The sun was beating down warmly, and the sea gulls were swooping overhead. "I was totally captured by the images of the story," she says. "There was no suspension of belief. I went with it completely, and it made me feel wonderful." Suddenly, she saw the slim volume, encased in a jacket of soaring sea gulls, in bookstore windows across the entire country.

As she sensed then, *Jonathan Livingston Seagull* was a story for adults, not children. At Friede's urging, Macmillan published it in 1970, but with a meager first printing scaled down from ten thousand to seventy-five hundred copies by the marketing department. Friede's Little Nothing Book, as it was called inside the publishing house, appeared in September without any reviews. Television talk show hosts, so important to book sales, declined to invite author Richard Bach, scoffing, "What are we going to talk about, sea gulls?" Nevertheless, the book sold out before Christmas. Even so, Macmillan was not inclined to reprint.

Friede pressed for a second printing right away, intuitively sensing that a *Jonathan Livingston Seagull* phenomenon could catch the country by surprise. Then suddenly the talk show invitations started to come, confirming her feeling. "As an editor, you're supposed to know if what's in your head is going to transfer to other people," she says. "I felt there were truths in this simple story that would make it an international classic."

The book has since sold 3.2 million copies in hard cover and 7 million in paperback. It has also been published in twenty-seven languages, including Eskimo. Adds Friede: "Too many forces came together all at once in the publication of *Jonathan* not to believe in the existence of some kind of a universal information matrix."

But a recitation of highly profitable hunches doesn't reveal the intuitive process. It doesn't explain this perceptive power that enables one individual to peer up into the night sky and see a faint star twinkling while equally intelligent colleagues see only the blackness.

The late business philosopher R. Buckminster Fuller, designer of the geodesic dome, called intuition "cosmic fishing." But he warned, "Once you feel a nibble, you've

got to hook the fish." Too many people, he said, "get a
hunch, then light up a cigarette and forget about it."

DEFINING INTUITION

What is this mystical power, magical facility, this guardian angel that is smarter than we are and can take care of us,
provided it is allowed to function? The athlete speaks of
mind and movement coalescing or, less poetically, of
eye-hand coordination. The Zen Buddhist describes the
sound of one hand clapping. The businessman talks about
his gut feeling. Their vocabularies differ, but their inner
messages have the same submerged origin.

Intuition is knowledge gained without rational thought.
And since it comes from some stratum of awareness just
below the conscious level, it is slippery and elusive, to say
the least. Under hypnosis the unconscious can recall incredible things that we have no idea are being collected. These
subconsciously perceived factors are sorted out and integrated into retained impressions that often can't even be
verbalized though they guide our actions.

Not being able to articulate a hazy, indistinct, subliminal
impression doesn't mean that it surfaced by accident. Or
that it was pulled from a void. New ideas spring from a
mind that organizes experiences, facts, and relationships to
discern a path that has not been taken before. Somewhere
along this uncharted path, intuition compresses years of
learning and experience into an instantaneous flash.

There's no guarantee that it's going to be a positive flash,
though that is usually the case. Some individuals instinctively invite negative feelings that become self-fulfilling
prophecies ("Everything I eat turns to fat"). The way
intuition operates, you tend to get what you ask yourself for.
Or as Joseph McKinney, chairman of the Tyler Corporation,
says: "Intuition works in proportion to need." He also talks
about "all that voltage down there in the subconscious."
But that high power has to be invoked. It has to be coaxed
into constructive use by desire. When confronted with what
seems like an insurmountable business problem, John

Fetzer, chairman of both the Detroit Tigers and the Fetzer Broadcasting Company, says: "I literally order my subconscious mind to do research and come up with some answers."

In thinking intuitively you may not realize you've asked for something. Dr. Benjamin Libet, a physiologist at the University of California in San Francisco who measures brain waves, claims that the brain begins to ask for something—and actually initiates the action—about four-tenths of a second before the brain's owner is aware of wanting it. So even the simplest voluntary actions may start deep in the subconscious, that dark, secret place where we harbor so many of our likes, dislikes, and desires.

So where does that first glimmer of a new concept, new product, new market, or new solution to a problem come from? Elusive as it is, we do know certain characteristics of this inner impression or hunch. It concerns relationships, involves simultaneous perception of a whole system, and can draw a conclusion—not necessarily correct—without proceeding through logical intermediary steps. That's why intuition comes with that queasy feeling of almost but not quite knowing.

Herman Kahn, a physicist turned futurist and director of the Hudson Institute until his death in 1983, said: "My research is a combination of intuition and judgment. I don't know where it comes from. The mind simply puts things together."

TESTING INTUITION

How the corporate chief's mind puts things together is being studied intensively by a handful of scientists and academicians. They have come up with measurable proof that subconscious elements play an important role in decision-making and have even discovered a correlation between the boss's precognitive power (the facility of deciphering telltale signs of the future) and the company's profitability. They point out that it isn't realistic for executives to rely solely on logic to cope with the complexities of modern business.

It is an explorer back from outer space, astronaut Edgar Mitchell, who has turned into one of intuition's most fervent evangelists. A doctor of science from MIT, a former navy captain, and the sixth man on the moon, Mitchell believes that man's potential knowledge is more than the product of his five senses.

Mitchell was obviously using two kinds of vision, seeing with both his physical eye and mind's eye, when he gazed back at our blue living planet from the dusty dead moon. From that distant vantage point he saw the earth's ills as curable only by intuition, and recalcitrantly incurable if mankind insists on sticking to a strictly analytical approach. He still speaks almost reverently of the "mysterious, creative process that works outside our conscious awareness," which he is convinced quietly remains available to help us solve our most difficult problems.

In preparing for a lunar flight, Mitchell explains, "We spent ten percent of our time studying plans for the mission and ninety percent learning how to react intuitively to all the 'what ifs.'" Reliance on the intuitive response, he claims, was the most important part of his astronaut's training.

Following his journey to the moon, Mitchell founded the Institute of Noetic Sciences ("noetic" is from a Greek word for intuitive knowing) in Sausalito, California. His aim is to help his fellow man—especially the businessman—develop intuitive decision-making powers to the point where, as Mitchell says, "we can control the scientific beast." Advocating use of a space-age spin-off called failure analysis, he believes that chief executives should interview managers, foremen, and workers to uncover their innate fears about all the things that can go wrong. Explains Mitchell: "With a computer printout of the resulting 'fault tree' in front of him, a boss can almost smell those failures before they occur." The disaster at Bhopal, India, might have been averted if Union Carbide had subjected itself to this kind of intuitive, "what if" failure analysis.

Intuition studies are already invading national defense.

Clandestine experiments involving the Pentagon and the psychic community have been going on for a few years to discover if the movement of Soviet submarines can be determined extrasensorally. The Defense Department has spent several million dollars on ESP and mental telepathy research, or what it calls Novel Biological Information Transfer Systems. Also being explored by the Pentagon is the far-out possibility of weapons systems that might somehow be triggered by the power of the mind.

Doctors, of course, have already found ways of harnessing psychic power to trigger body changes. Biofeedback has certainly proved helpful in the healing process, though many executives may still consider it just short of sorcery. And while self-proclaimed psychics keep popping up all over the place, insisting that they can remove diseased organs—or for that matter, bend metal or project photographic images—by using nothing more than intense concentration, the business leader quite understandably shrinks from being associated with such kooks.

But society's current addiction to psychic advice is hardly what executives mean when they secretly admit to following hunches. To the businessman or woman, words like "precognitive" and "psychic" smack of the occult. But suggest to this same sophisticated leader—not only in business, but in sports, science, or the arts—that he or she might indeed possess certain intuitive powers that could be of real assistance in generating ideas, choosing alternative courses of action, and picking people, and you'll elicit a rapt response. At least that was true of the people interviewed for this book.

Such a response is not surprising. Today's decision-makers live intensely and have more obligations and money than they have time. For them the highest need is to cut through the complexities of the modern world and come to quick creative decisions intuitively. This book is designed to help identify, unlock, use, stimulate, and sometimes also temper business intuition, "that which is imprinted on the spirit of man(ager)," to borrow from the farseeing seventeenth-century British philosopher Francis Bacon.

Merely recognizing the existence of intuition is a positive first step. This means having faith in the fact that answers to the toughest problems can leap fully conceived into our awareness—and at the most unpropitious moment, as happened to Archimedes in the bath. But this amorphous, ill-defined instinct known as intuition has to be understood, nurtured, and trusted if it is to be turned into a powerful management tool.

2

THE ENEMY OF INTUITION

BIG organizations, and that includes governments, unions, and corporate oligopolies that submerge the individual, are clearly intuition's enemy. No boss can keep personal contact with everything going on, much less see down into the engine room of the organization where a head of antimanagement steam may even be building. Communication from below is expressed impersonally in numbers, plans, and analyses, and executive decisions are based on these abstractions. True enough, with a fine-tuned CEO, a Ronald Reagan, a Lane Kirkland, or a Lee Iacocca at the helm, a lot of gut feeling may flow down from on high. But on lower levels, intuitive ideas are automatically tuned out. Eurekas are simply not a factor, because no credence is given to anything that can't be weighed, measured, and analyzed by computer. So callow neophytes looking up from the bottom rung of the executive ladder are here forewarned about falling into these bureaucratic bear traps.

IDENTIFYING THE ARTICULATE INCOMPETENT

In smaller organizations, too, there is an unsuspected enemy whose deceptive mien threatens everyone, not just the free spirits around the place. "The articulate incompetent" is how Robert Bernstein, chairman of Random House, identifies the culprit. "Particularly in a business that depends on people and not machinery," says Bernstein, "only intuition can protect you against this most dangerous individual of all."

It's the B-school-glib, number-crunching fast-tracker, whose insights come from classroom case studies, about whom Bernstein is warning us. "That's what frightens me about business school," he says. "They train their students to sound wonderful. But it's necessary to find out if there's judgment behind their language."

The Random House chairman suggests a couple of ways, besides relying totally on intuition, to guard against articulate incompetents' infiltrating a company. "Watch out for résumés," he advises. "The best résumés don't produce the best people." He also suggests spurning the headhunter's siren song, sung to business leaders looking for help as well as to restless underlings seeking a loftier post. "We've never hired anyone from an executive search firm," Bernstein boasts. Additionally, he urges intuition be used in scanning term papers, particularly masters' and doctoral theses, as samples of a job applicant's ability. "Quality bullshit," he calls that kind of writing.

Mary Kay Ash describes how she was almost disastrously hoodwinked by an articulate incompetent during the launch of her cosmetics company back in 1963. "We were starting out with nine people," she says. "Eight women and one man. The women were inexperienced. But the man sounded like a marketing whiz, spouting enthusiastic plans for getting Mary Kay Cosmetics off the ground. I had already promised to hire him. But as I stood talking to the man outside the office, I suddenly changed my mind," recalls the impetuous entrepreneuse. "I had no reason. Just intuition. Six months later I read in the newspaper that he had been indicted on a felony."

Of course, it isn't about crooks that Bernstein is cautioning us, but leftover members of the me generation and their high-consuming Young Upwardly Mobile Professional successors. They are the nemesis of the intuitive manager. For yumpies and their hedonistic urban yuppie cousins, anything that can't be tasted, smelled, or seen simply doesn't exist. Their main invasion route into the executive suite is easy enough to trace. It begins in B-school, banks steeply around the ranks of the campus recruiters, climbs rapidly over the headhunter-infested foothills, and if all goes according to plan, winds up at the corporate pinnacle.

Fortunately, travelers on this fast track are easy to spot, spouting hyphenated buzzwords like "cost-benefits," "bidding-games," and "decision-trees," and seeming to identify with a few of their favorite books. "We're *The Best and the Brightest*," they're frank to admit. That they're *Looking Out for Number One* comes across equally loud and clear, as they switch companies, houses, and mates *In Search of Excellence*. Almost one out of three employed managers in the United States has a résumé making the rounds, reports National Personnel Associates, a network of independent recruiters. Obviously, to the Young Upwardly Mobile Professional the pile carpet looks deeper in the other company's executive suite.

The anti-intuitive behavior pattern of these fast-trackers has already been enumerated by several pop-psych specialists, who claim yumpies and yuppies are too frenetically busy to think deeply and give any subconscious creativity a chance to float to the surface. Their days alternate between nerve-wracking work and bone-tiring play. *Preppy Handbook* editor Lisa Birnbach says these ambitious young men and women are attempting to become the generation of the *Übermensch* and *Übermenschette*. "The only women I know who don't work," she says, "are those who are actually on the delivery table."

There is nothing very intuitive, either, in the way fast-trackers go about picking a job. Demonstrating excessive security needs, they give precedence to contract-signing bonuses, fringe benefits, and stock option plans. They prefer neatly structured businesses to creative environments and are deadly serious, shunning the kind of playfulness in the workplace that often induces intuition.

Surprisingly, fast-trackers also secretly fear change unless it shows promise of catapulting them into a position of enhanced power. EDS chairman Ross Perot says he has been invited to the Harvard Business School occasionally to talk to the students before they invade industry and commerce. "I tell them that I give HBS an A-plus for the young people it attracts, but an F for what it does to them while they're there. 'In due course you'll shrug off this experience and go out and be successful," he adds. "By this time I have their attention. The gist of my speech is that if they don't come out of school and get dirty, they won't learn the skills they need to become intuitive managers."

OTHER INTUITION BLOCKERS

But not all of the prevailing anti-intuitive feeling in business stems from these B-school invaders. Some of it results from today's business environment, especially in steel, cars, and oil. If the key players in these industries aren't staving off the Japanese, OPEC, or an onslaught of robots, they are out trying to ambush each other. Corporate raiders may be highly intuitive in selecting and stalking their prey. But the hurly-burly of tender offers, leveraged buyouts, white knights, and greenmail is not conducive to the thoughtful contemplation that produces great insights.

Internally, too, many enterprises abound in misconceptions that further curtail the use of intuition. Computer forecasting is rarely as accurate as its practitioners would have you believe. Meetings supposedly stimulate brainstorming, though psychiatrists say the gamesmanship that goes on is an intuition blocker.

Another popular misconception is the belief that good analyses and good outcomes are synonymous. The former simply means the problem has been diagnosed correctly. As might be expected, the articulate incompetent's impressive analysis doesn't automatically produce good results.

Abraham Zaleznik, a psychoanalyst and the Konosuke Matsushita Professor of Leadership at the Harvard Business School, cites what he claims was a classic example of deceptive analysis. "Xerox," he says, "couldn't figure out what else to do in its own office machine field, so it got into somebody else's—insurance."

In 1982, after an intensive nine-month study, Xerox

Corporation paid $1.6 billion in cash and stock to acquire Crum & Forster, a property and casualty company. The diversification move confused Wall Street analysts, who wondered if Xerox was getting out of the office equipment business. Besides, the price paid for C&F exceeded the fair value of the insurance company's net assets by $943 million. Nevertheless, Xerox's chief executive, David Kearns, termed the acquisition "a highly aggressive approach to make Xerox a stronger company. It's the beginning of another jewel," he said. But fierce price-cutting in the property and casualty insurance market shrank C&F's earnings and helped send Xerox stock into a tailspin.

CORROSIVE CHEMISTRY

Zaleznik further believes that today's trend of appointing uncharismatic chief financial officers and general counsels as CEO's is putting an added damper on intuitive decision-making. Because the CEO's personal chemistry (particularly accountants and lawyers who become boss) can be highly corrosive, eating into the creativity of subordinates, a new mini-industry has sprung up consisting of management consultants who specialize in prescribing neutralizing procedures.

The clearest clues to executives' chemistry, these consultants claim, lie in the origins of the people involved. Cultural background, education, regional habits—all naturally contribute to personal values. So does the side of the business they grow up on, which explains the allergic reaction that can flare up between sales-oriented marketing directors and cost-oriented financial managers. Some corporations try to pick personality types at the top to strike a productive balance. Federated Department Stores has for some time tried to build "positive interaction" into its management appointments. Its policy is to match imaginative merchandisers with cold-eyed bean-counters as chairman and president of each division—unless, as one former Federated executive says, "the tangling between the two tigers gets out of hand. Then the team is broken up."

Another clue to an executive's chemistry is what in business school jargon is called T-M balance, the mixture of technical and managerial experience in the person's career. People who make their mark as inventors or technicians sometimes have trouble adjusting to the sophisticated nuances of upper management. That's why the entrepreneurial founder often gives way to the professional manager who is brought in to help the company expand.

In many cases, the highly charged chemistry in a company is never reduced to words. In his book *Body Language,* Julius Fast used the term "kinesics" to describe those almost imperceptible reflexes that speak louder than words. He points out that some bosses, throwbacks to more autocratic days in business, use the arched eyebrow, the stiffened posture in a chair, or the time it takes them to answer a knock on their office door to reinforce that "you work for me" relationship. Anthropologist Edward T. Hall, in his book *The Hidden Dimension,* invented the term "proxemics" to describe man's manipulation of the space around him for sending domineering signals.

The acid that most commonly curdles working relationships is pride: the belief that one's ability and creativity are not being used. Feeling unappreciated is a terrible intuition suppressor. Yet today, American business is presumably in its most participatory period. The boss's autocratic hand has been relaxed. Power has been decentralized. The new spirit that management is trying to foster is individual resourcefulness, not lockstep compliance. However, this doesn't mean that all big and intimidating business organizations are automatically loosening their bonds.

SPAWNING CREATIVITY

It takes a perceptive CEO, oftentimes one who remembers how freewheeling and exciting things were during his company's start-up days, to initiate remedial action. Nevertheless, any intuitive CEO can implement certain changes to help make the biggest corporation more sensitive to its creative people. Establishing autonomous subunits with their own budgets and profit centers encourages inventive, entrepreneurial spirit to bubble up from the bottom, and may even spark an occasional Eureka. The term "intrapreneurship," now in vogue, describes the setting up of small separate businesses within such behemoths as GM or IBM so talented employees can chase their dreams and possibly strike it rich without quitting.

In Silicon Valley, especially, engineering jobs grow like oranges and loyalty is to the magical powers of the microprocessor, not to the companies that make them. Action there is being taken to keep the most promising idea people from jumping around the employment orchard. Hewlett-Packard, for one, makes sure that its people share in the successes they create. Profit sharing and decentralized operating control are H-P's secret weapons. Each division also does its own research. "That way, nobody has to come hat in hand begging for R-and-D money," explained cofounder and chairman David Packard, one of the valley's richest entrepreneurs and an intuitive boss who never forgot his company's humble beginnings.

Offering special recognition is another way of rewarding creativity. Charles House won H-P's "medal of defiance" for pursuing an idea for an advanced picture tube despite a kill order from management. The tube was eventually used for the moon lander's monitor, enabling all of us earthlings to see a clear picture of the first man on the moon.

Besides honorary awards, recognition may consist of titles, trips, and anniversary parties. Or it may simply come in the form of a compliment. But it takes an intuitive boss to know when praise is needed. In the vernacular of the management consultant, BLT (bright lights and trumpets) is the best recognition sandwich. Of course, autonomy also allows room for failure, important in the maturing process of any manager. Failures, as well as successes, become etched in the mind of every individual and help adjust that subconscious compass called intuition.

Since loyalty, like an elevator, runs down as well as up, there are a number of other buttons the intuitive CEO (chief elevator operator) must push to make it work. These include accessibility and listening ability on the part of upper management, as well as quick internal communications, a channel for expressing dissent, and a reliable performance evaluation system. Without them the boss's best intentions may get stuck between floors.

In Japan, where corporate loyalty borders on the mystical, it is said: "Man, not the bottom line, is the measure of all things." Boss and worker both are valued for their uniqueness as human beings, and a close intuitive bond exists between them. The same idea may be taking root here. A recent study indicates that Japanese companies transplanted to U.S. soil are outperforming their American rivals.

Still, plenty of creative young careerists inadvertently find themselves plugging away in big, unresponsive companies, just as many articulate incompetents slip through the human resources net and get hired. But AI (articulate incompetency) may be curable.

Eugene Jennings, a Michigan State University Business School professor, thinks time and experience do cure it. He is in a position to see the problem from two sides. Besides his days spent in academia, Jennings also works as a business consultant, or what he calls "a counselor to chairmen and presidents in trouble." He states that it takes B-school grads about five years to "wash the academic training out of their hair." That's about the same amount of time, he claims, that it takes a new doctor "to realize he's treating the whole patient and not just one organ." Of course, Jennings is assuming that the business or medical intern had an intuitive mind to begin with. "Analysis," he says, "does not wipe out intuition forever. As any psychologist will tell you, the intuitive mind is far stronger than the analytical mind."

In any case, the professor believes that the dichotomy between intuition and analysis is more imagined than real. He claims that "historically, the best, though highly individual American business leaders—the Robert Woodses, Alfred Sloans, and Tom Watsons—had one thing in common. Their heads and hearts were usually working together." But, adds Jennings, "these leaders had good sniffers."

Without a good sniffer, Jennings believes, a boss doesn't know if he's being snowed by analysis. At the same time, without proper respect for analysis, his gut reaction may be wrong. "When an intuitive leader's head and heart don't agree, he'll go back to the drawing board," Jennings says. However, the professor points out, less balanced chief executives "tend to coerce the facts to fit their feelings." And that, he claims, "can create a Bay of Pigs problem right away."

3

MONITOR VERSUS MOVER

WHEN Professor Jennings speaks of a chief executive's head and heart working together, he's really talking about what's going on in both sides of the boss's brain. As scientists have recently determined, the right hemisphere of the brain provides the creative impulse and is the decision-maker's prime mover, while the left hemisphere handles the logical, linear functions and serves as the decision-maker's monitor. Mover and Monitor are often in conflict. Monitor usually tries to encroach upon Mover by forcing it to face facts, follow a strict deadline, or by stifling Mover's unquantifiable feelings.

Until just a few years ago this whole concept of brain-hemisphere specialization, to say nothing of its importance in business, was not realized. Doctors had only vague notions of how man's bicameral command center worked. Removed from its protective shell and viewed from above, the three-and-a-half-pound brain was described as looking like a big walnut, cleaved down the middle. But the manner in which these twin segments harmonized was a matter for medical conjecture.

Hippocrates, whose oath is still being administered to medical school graduates, suspected correctly more than two thousand years ago that the right half controls the left side of the body and vice versa. He noticed that sword wounds on one side of the head affected movements on the other side of the body. Eventually, in 1861, a French physician, Paul Broca, discovered that injuries only to the left side of the head caused speech disorders, indicating that the two brain hemispheres, or lobes, as they are sometimes called, also performed different mental functions.

It was finally Roger Sperry, a bearded, bullet-eyed psychobiologist at Caltech, who sorted out the various right- and left-brain specialties, and as a result he shared the 1981 Nobel Prize in physiology or medicine. "In many respects," wrote Sperry, "each hemisphere appears to have a separate 'mind of its own.'" But he also found that the two sides can, indeed, collaborate on certain tasks, since they are connected by the corpus callosum, a sort of coaxial cable consisting of some 200 million nerve fibers. It was by testing epileptics whose corpus callosum had been surgically cut to reduce the intensity of their seizures that Sperry isolated the functions of each hemisphere.

VERBAL VERSUS VISUAL

The pioneering Sperry and his followers determined that Monitor, the left hemisphere, specializes in verbal, quantitative, and analytical work—the kind of mental effort that goes into preparing a planning report—while Mover, the right hemisphere, is more visually, artistically, and intuitively adroit, and therefore more useful in creating new products or in seizing on new business opportunities.

Business schools, of course, still put heavy emphasis on developing left-brain talents. Courses like Harvard's Applied Data Analysis, Marketing Decision Support Systems, and Ethical Aspects of Corporate Policy bear witness to that. Surprisingly, the HBS catalogue now also lists what appears to be a right-brain special: Power and Insolence. Described as "an important challenge for those aspiring to hold positions of considerable managerial authority," this course is said to focus on "power, power motives, and power skills, and how those intrapsychic factors affect a person's behavior." The course summary also promises to "help students learn how to deal with these issues in ways that are socially responsible, organizationally effective, and"—thank goodness—"personally nondestructive."

As a result of most business school training, the articulate incompetent may simply be suffering from acute left-lobitis. But then, as Sperry came to appreciate, Western culture has consistently stacked the educational deck in favor of what was believed to be the "dominant" left hemisphere.

As Sperry's experiments progressed, he became convinced that the so-called mute, nonverbal right side of the brain was vastly undervalued. Its sensory prowess, he saw, imbued a person with superior problem-solving capabilities, particularly in situations where a single impression or mental image is worth a thousand carefully crafted words. He coined the term "left-brained" to connote the careful, plodding type, the kind of pin-striped subordinate who can rise to rock-solid executive VP but isn't enough of a visionary to run the company.

THE TWO CAN WORK IN TANDEM

The lesson of all this for business leaders is, don't let the left, monitoring side of your brain overanalyze problems or talk you out of moving intuitively into an exciting new venture. Better yet, get Monitor and Mover working in tandem to avoid an impetuous decision. Remember Adam and the Apple—not the biblical story, but a made-up, modern-day parable of right- and left-hemisphere prowess.

Adam Osborne has been a persistent right-brained rebel, a chip off his British countermissionary father, who converted Burmese tribesmen back from Christianity to Buddhism. Holding a doctorate in chemical engineering, Adam quit his job at one of Shell's cracking plants to launch a consulting business. He wrote the original best-seller on microprocessing, then launched a publishing company that produced books about computers, which McGraw-Hill quickly bought out for $4 million. With this money he produced the first practical personal computer in 1981, managing to market it, complete with software, for a bargain $1,800. Some seventy-five thousand Osborne PCs were sold that first year, enriching Adam enormously.

But at this point, instead of seeking a little left-brained

surveillance of competitors entering the then Eden-like marketplace, or implementing an accounting system to monitor the expenses that were being racked up by the droves of temporary employees he had taken on to meet the initial surge of orders, Adam plunged ahead. He also committed the "original sin" of his industry—disclosing plans for a new model before he had a salable product. So demand for the existing models quickly dried up, and Adam's company went belly-up.

In the same way, the Apple computer would have remained in a Silicon Valley garage without the right-brain impetus of young Steven Jobs. But Jobs, unlike Osborne, realized that he needed a new, carefully orchestrated, left-brained marketing strategy once he got his company going, and he hired professional manager John Sculley away from PepsiCo to be president and implement one. Jobs remained chairman, relegating himself to the dual role of "guardian of Apple's spirit" and "intuitor of future products." Later, however, he tried to depose Sculley, who then pulled the plug on Jobs, kicking him upstairs to be "global visionary." Jobs quit to launch another computer company, although he remains Apple's biggest stockholder. You might wonder what prompts the author to link Adam and the Apple computer together in this book. Ah, but a writer's fertile right brain can't resist joining disparate elements to drive home a point.

Some executives appear to be cerebrally ambidextrous, able to call on either hemisphere as the situation requires. In a speech to students of that left-brain bastion the Harvard Business School, Seagram's chairman Edgar Bronfman recalled how during the heat of the takeover battle for Conoco, his brother Charles asked him: "How do the figures look?" Replied Edgar, who prides himself on being highly intuitive as well as something of a number-cruncher: "Whatever scenario you want, I can deliver. The figures can look bad, so-so, or great. It depends on the assumptions used."

Seagram didn't end up acquiring Conoco. But it did emerge from the battle owning 21 percent of Du Pont's stock, obtained in exchange for the Conoco shares Seagram had accumulated. Bronfman also confided to the students that Seagram's investment bankers (a predominantly left-brained profession) had initially argued against challenging mighty Du Pont, although Seagram's war spoils ended up at $2.26 billion.

"I had a gut feeling for my assumptions," Bronfman said. "That doesn't mean I use a crystal ball or smoke opium. It just means that I have a point of view based on all the data fed into my personal computer—my brain—where they mix with my instincts, my vibes, my experience."

Rudyard Kipling described that same kind of coolness under fire when he wrote about the importance of keeping one's head "while all about are losing theirs." But then Kipling was highly appreciative of the double-barreled brain God had endowed him with. More than a half century ago he wrote:

> Much I owe to the Lands that grew—
> More to the Lives that fed—
> But most to Allah Who gave me two
> Separate sides to my head.

THE ELUSIVE RIGHT-BRAIN STUFF

Many writers since Kipling have struggled to glorify the specialized missions of the separate sides of their head. The "pristine innocence of perception" is how a poetic psychologist describes the right brain's fruitful insight, breadth and depth of mental association, and its ability to screen out the seemingly irrelevant.

But the mute right hemisphere can't even verbalize what it senses about itself, though by nature it's a mighty good guesser. The plodding left hemisphere, on the other hand, gathers all kinds of detail about everything, including the brain, and is vocal to boot. Still, it doesn't see the big picture. So relying on this two-sided information service to find out what's going on inside our heads is like trying to piece together the words of a loquacious but blind reporter and the views of a tongue-tied seer.

In *The Book of Floating*, author Michael Hutchison advocates resting suspended in a flotation tank for an hour or so as the most efficient means of gaining access to the contents of the right hemisphere. "In recent years," he writes,

> many have recognized the dangers of left-hemisphere dominance and have undertaken various ways to emphasize the right-brain functions. Meditation, yoga, Zen, consciousness-altering drugs, chanting, dancing, running, guided dreaming, visualization, self-hypnosis, and many other techniques have been used to open up the right hemisphere.

But nothing, Hutchison claims, works as well as simply floating in a tank of water.

Perhaps an explanation of the right brain's true power will forever elude us. The Eastern mystics believe that to explain something means to show how it is ultimately connected to everything else. Since this is impossible, they insist that no single phenomenon can be explained. As the ancient Buddhist sage Aśvaghosa said: "All things in their fundamental nature are not nameable or explicable. They cannot be adequately expressed in any form of language."

For modern-day executives, the important thing is not to let the opposite, monitoring side of the brain denounce those inexplicable insights as being impractical. Alex Osborn, a former principal in the ad agency Batten Barton Durstine & Osborn, was the first businessman to make practical progress in the war against left-brain dominance. An educator by training, he was mystified by why some people in his agency were so creative whole others came up with nothing. That was back in the 1930s, long before Roger Sperry's experiments. But even then Osborn concluded that people had two modes of thought, one acting as an "idea generator," the other acting as an "idea filter." His solution was to eliminate the filter.

Gathering the BBD&O creative staff together, Osborn would toss out a problem and ask everybody in the room to mention anything that came to mind, no matter how ridiculous it sounded. He silenced critical remarks by ringing a bell. Instead of coming up with 5 or 6 ideas in an hour, the roomful of people soon were generating up to 150. Judgment was deferred until later. "Brainstorming" was the term Osborn coined to describe the technique that became standard procedure at the agency and eventually spread to other business organizations.

Today it still bodes well for executives to ring a mental bell, and to be wary of the left brain's monitoring role. The left hemisphere analyzes by breaking things down into components or step-by-step progressions—the kind of thinking consultants provide. But it doesn't soar *Jonathan Livingston Seagull*-style to a bright new vision.

THE CEO'S BUTTERFLY BRAIN

Sperry and his followers never said that one side of the brain is switched off while the other side is switched on. He indicated that the two hemispheres seem capable of constructive cooperation. But how the two sides focus on a single objective is still a mystery. Do the brain hemispheres turn on simultaneously, or alternate like electric current? Random House's Robert Bernstein, who relies heavily on his intuition, admits: "I have a butterfly brain that flits from one idea to another"—and apparently back and forth from one hemisphere to the other.

There is, in fact, considerable evidence that many CEOs have butterfly brains, or at least that the superanalytical creature pictured at the corporate pinnacle is so much "folklore." That, anyway, is the view of Professor Henry Mintzberg of the McGill University Faculty of Management, who has been dissecting and writing about the executive animal for many years.

Ever since he became aware of Dr. Sperry's split-brain studies at Caltech, Mintzberg has been fascinated with the notion that the analytical, planning functions in business might best be separated from the creative management functions. In an article titled "Planning on the Left Side and Managing on the Right," published by the *Harvard Business Review* in 1976, Mintzberg first broached the revolutionary idea that students of business may have been mistakenly "looking for the key to management in the lightness of logical analysis," while perhaps it has "been lost in the darkness of intuition." Specifically, he proposed that "there may be a fundamental difference between formal planning and informal managing, akin to that between the two hemispheres of the human brain."

According to Mintzberg (who appropriately is the Bronfman Professor of Management at McGill) the CEO merely pays lip service to systematic long-range planning, elaborate tables of organization, and reliance on computers and esoteric quantitative techniques ("more folklore"). In reality, he's a "holistic intuitive thinker who revels in a climate of calculated chaos." Mintzberg portrays the CEO as working at an unrelenting pace, jumping from topic to topic, disposing of items in ten minutes or less, and "constantly relying on hunches to cope with problems far too complex for rational analysis."

No criticism intended. The puckish professor has immense admiration for the CEO's innate sense of direction, which he claims is much more reliable than that of the analytical consultant who is forever devising inflexible guidance systems for unmapped business terrain. "After all," says Mintzberg, "the intuitive Eskimo crosses the ice cap without a compass."

The intuitive executive, he explains, solves problems in four interrelated stages set forth in Gestalt psychology. In case college days are a bit behind you and the lessons of Psych I have faded, Gestalt is the German school of psychology which maintains that the structured whole is more than the sum of the separate parts, and is analogous to the quantum-field theory in physics. The four stages, as described by Mintzberg, are: preparation ("creativity favors the prepared mind"); incubation ("letting the subconscious do the work"); illumination ("waking up in the middle of the night and shouting, 'Eureka, I've got it!' ''); and verification ("then working it all out linearly"). These four crucial steps for inducing and verifying intuition will be dealt with in the next four parts of this book.

II
PREPARATION

4

"THE VAPOR OF PAST EXPERIENCES"

ENRICHING intuition's seedbed is a mixture of vague recollections, incongruous observations, and hazy judgments of events gone by. However indistinct, they hark back to a host of specific failures and successes, the sum of a lifetime's living. That's why Joyce C. Hall, the mystical founder of the Hallmark Company, the firm that today generates millions of words (and $3.2 billion in annual revenues) of greetings for every occasion, called intuition "the vapor of past experiences."

If the subconscious mix causing this vapor is right, it can result in the glimmer of a new idea. A loose connection forms between things thought to be unrelated. Perceived first only faintly, the idea may become much more strongly sensed. The sensation of homing in on something is often felt.

At the same time, thoughts and images stemming strictly from memory are called "mental noise" by psychologists. They claim it interferes with intuition, since memorized information tends to produce preconceived views. Intuitive impressions stemming from visceral learning, they say, are more gentle and fleeting and can be drowned out by mental noise. Although these intuitive impressions appear spontaneously and can't be summoned on command like memorized information, certain self-imposed attitudes and conditions can help create them.

BUILDING MENTAL MODELS

Joseph McKinney, before his tenure as chairman of the Tyler Corporation, became a millionaire by the time he was twenty-nine investing in high-tech long shots. Three years later the former St. Joseph's College basketball star and Harvard Business School scholarship student found himself plunged almost into bankruptcy.

In the depth of his depression he became fascinated by a book with the tongue-twisting title *Psycho-Cybernetics*. The author, Dr. Maxwell Maltz, now dead, was a noted plastic surgeon and became a friend of McKinney's. In the course of his career Maltz was astonished to find that improving the facial appearance of patients didn't necessarily improve their self-image, so crucial for attaining success. Seeking an explanation, he pursued the study of cybernetics (the goal-seeking behavior of mechanical systems). The plastic surgeon concluded that there is a success mechanism deep down in the subconscious that will intuitively steer an individual to a desired objective—provided the individual has a vivid mental picture of his ultimate victory and doesn't jam the defense mechanism with fear and doubt.

Armed with this faith, McKinney began assembling the components that evolved into the Tyler Corporation—which now produces pipe, electronic parts, chemical coatings, and industrial explosives. "In business," he says, "I've found it's important to think of goals not as the means to an end, but as having already been accomplished. Like Daniel Boone walking through the wilderness, having a clear destination in mind makes you receptive to every little sign. You can be victimized by a false clue, of course. But an intuitive manager knows from a combination of clues when he's surrounded by Indians" (i.e., articulate incompetents).

Professor Henry Mintzberg claims that good managers create much more elaborate mental images for themselves than either Maltz or McKinney describes, and can envision a lot more looming ahead than just their personal success.

They "build mental models of their entire world," which Mintzberg says are "synthesized pictures" of how their companies and industries function. Then when the manager anticipates embarking on a new, uncharted path, he can project the outcome on the basis of the model.

But CEOs often construct this mental model in the most chaotic fashion. Reports the McGill University professor: "Clearly the manager does not operate in a systematic, orderly, intellectual way, puffing his pipe in a mountain retreat, as he analyzes his problems. Rather, he deals with issues in the context of his daily activities—a cigarette in his mouth, one hand on the telephone, and the other shaking hands with a departing guest. The manager is involved, plugged in. His mode of operating is relational, simultaneous, experiential, encompassing all the characteristics of the right hemisphere."

A leader's capacity to integrate such a rich mixture of sensory experiences cannot be taught and may not even be detectable. Neither can management science delineate all the roles executives must assume in obtaining this stream of impulses. Sometimes the boss must be a scientist, reorganizing the corporation's research and development department; at other times, an artist, picking the architectural design for the new headquarters.

STAYING ON TIME AND ON TRACK

In the welter of daily activities, a chief executive may lose sight of his goals. As Edgar Bronfman, Seagram's CEO, says: "When you're up to your neck in alligators, it's easy to forget that you started out to drain the swamp." Leaders need time to restudy their objectives. Yet time is something they don't have

Captives of their corporations and communities as well, many CEOs feel their time belongs to everybody else. They also complain that as they perform under today's tyranny of urgency, it is the recurring crisis rather than the creative side of business that swallows up their time. But for intuition to work, if only as a course-corrector in the pursuit of established goals, some quiet, contemplative time must be set aside. Otherwise, flying by the seat of their pants in all day-to-day decisions, chief executives come to find they are flying blind. At McDonald's Oak Brook, Illinois, headquarters, where offices are open cubicles and Ray Kroc's shouting used to ring through them, he established an elaborate "think tank" with a seven-hundred-gallon water-bed, where he or his aides could steal some peace and quiet to do their planning.

"When a CEO proclaims proudly that half of his time is discretionary, that probably means he has no idea where it goes," says Peter Drucker, professor of social science at Claremont Graduate School in California and author of numerous books on management techniques. Drucker admits that to "know thyself" may be an impossible task for us mortals. But all executives, he insists, should follow the injunction "Know thy time," though he is not optimistic that they ever will. "Thinking through priorities is what's important," he adds.

SETTING GOALS AND PRIORITIES

To counter the chaos in their daily schedule, CEOs are advised by consultants who specialize in conducting executive time studies to write down a series of goals—lifetime, three-year, and six-month goals. Even though intuition may propel the boss off in a totally unexpected direction, it helps to start out on a planned path, these experts agree.

"Don't be afraid to include such far-out wishes as losing forty pounds," recommends Alan Lakein, author of *How to Get Control of Your Time and Your Life*, "or such uncensored fantasies as climbing the Matterhorn." Executives, he feels, should identify both their "internal prime time" (when they do their clearest thinking) and their "external prime time" (the best time for dealing with others). These prime times should be used for pursuing their highest-priority goals.

"Priorities" has always been the byword of Donald Rumsfeld, chairman of G.D. Searle & Company until it was

taken over by Monsanto in 1985. His early career took him
from navy pilot to congressman and then to NATO ambas-
sador. Later, as Gerald Ford's White House chief of staff,
he wrote the following reminder to himself: "Control your
own time. Don't let it be done for you. If you are working
off the in-box that is fed to you, you are probably working
on the priority of others."

But Rumsfeld found his own maxim impossible to follow
after he became Secretary of Defense. "The time demands
on the head of a big government bureaucracy are much
greater than on a business leader," he says. "It's part of the
political charade of seeming to do everything yourself."
Particularly disruptive to his contemplative process in the
Pentagon was the sheer weight of the facts and figures
(mental noise) spewed out by the military services. "It's like
drinking out of a fire hose, there's such a flood of
information," he says.

Since leaving the government, Rumsfeld maintains, he
has had more opportunity to think and be reflective, though
after observing him in motion, that was hard to confirm.
"At Searle," he says, "I was judged by results rather than
by appearances, so I could keep better control of my time."

Was it a gut feeling that catapulted this priority-conscious
man out of politics and into the boss's chair at G.D. Searle?
"Life is never what one plans," Rumsfeld admits. "You've
got to look backward and forward and see how you're
spending it." (John Lennon, the murdered rock star, expressed this same thought a little differently in a ballad:
"Life is what happens to you while you're busy making
other plans.")

LETTING LIFELONG URGES SURFACE

An intuitive entrepreneur who dramatically reset his
goals some years ago is Stephen Lieber, founder and
president of the Evergreen funds. Formerly a partner in a
large Wall Street firm, he became convinced that "a lot of
people could manage a lot of money bureaucratically and

badly. Or a few people with close communications and time to think could manage a lot of money very well."

In 1971 he abandoned Wall Street and formed Lieber & Company ("an investment think tank," he calls it) in Harrison, New York. The move also involved a life-style change. "I wanted to live in a more contemplative, less pressured way," he says. Lieber and his band of young investment advisers ("I feel as if I'm their professor") began seeking out either small, profitable companies with a unique nationally marketed product, or regional businesses with a lock on their local communities. "Some people get swallowed up in facts," he says. "What I do sometimes surprises my young colleagues. I make investment decisions that appear to be based on a shallow survey. But experience has made me familiar with the underlying pattern. A small sample will give me the trend. And I'll take the gamble on the sample." What Lieber fails to mention is that his gambles are backed by years in the investment business and a lifetime goal.

In most instances, Lieber claims, his "analytical decisions and intuitive leaps are not in opposition." Anyway, his system seems to be working. The investments managed by his company grew so rapidly that he launched two no-load mutual funds (Evergreen Fund and Evergreen Total Return Fund). For the ten-year period ending March 1985, the Evergreen Fund showed the biggest gain (1,091 percent) of the sixty-three funds appearing in *Money* magazine's list of maximum capital gains funds. "I had no intention of getting into the mutual fund business," says Lieber. "But it has proved to be the key to our success.

Debbi Fields, president and CEO of Mrs. Fields Cookies, which has over two hundred stores scattered around the United States, Asia, and Australia, says she always felt "an emotional need to bake cookies and make people happy." But she had no notion how far this feeling would carry her. "As a teenager," she says, "I became well known for having tons of cookies at home. But when I told some friends who worked for Procter & Gamble and General

Mills that I wanted to go into the cookie business, they said it was a terrible idea."

In 1977, at the age of twenty, Debbi opened a cookie shop in Palo Alto, California. "I only wanted one store," she says, "but I wanted to make it a personal statement of what I thought about quality, service, and the way a business should be run." The first day, when no customers appeared, she picked up a sheet of cookies and marched down the street, proferring them to passersby. "'Would you please try one?'" I said. It didn't dawn on me that wasn't the way to start a business. But intuitively it seemed the right thing to do." The 1985 sales of Mrs. Fields Cookies will top $30 million.

On the other hand, Mary Kay Ash never did plan to enter the cosmetics business. In 1963 she decided to retire after a lackluster career spent in the middle management of a number of catalogue sales companies. "I felt there were many women like me who were qualified to do a lot more than they were doing," she says. "My idea was to write a book that would help them over the obstacles I had encountered. But I didn't know how to write a book."

As a preliminary step she spent three weeks jotting down on one legal pad all of the business practices she felt stymied women's advancement. Then on a second pad she enumerated those practices that she felt were helpful and worth emulating. "Inadvertently," she says, "I had put on paper the marketing plan for a company that would give women an open-ended opportunity. My plan spelled out in black and white how they could climb from one rung up to the next."

Those yellow pads turned out to be not the fodder for a book but the business prospectus of Mary Kay Cosmetics. "The mental exercise of preparing all those notes sparked my impulse to start a marketing company," she says. But how she hit upon the skin care was also accidental.

"To launch a marketing company, I realized that I would need a product so good consumers would reach out to buy it," she recalls. For ten years she had been using a wonderful skin cream that a hide tanner had concocted to soften his hands after exposing them to the harsh chemicals used in his trade. When the tanner died, his daughter continued producing the cream in her garage and selling it to friends. But the woman had no idea how to really market the product. So Mary Kay Ash, who had discovered that the cream made her own skin look much younger, bought the secret formula.

Now a great-grandmother, she reigns over a $300 million-a-year empire that includes 1,500 employees and 150,000 "skin-care consultants," to whom she has awarded some two thousand pink Cadillacs, or "trophies on wheels," as she calls them. And she finally did write that book: *Mary Kay on People Management*. "Sensing how people will react," she says, is her forte.

Those vapors of past experience that materialized into Mary Kay Ash's highly profitable hunch also gave wings to Federal Express. Frederick Smith was a student at Yale when he first got the idea of reversing the old business maxim about building a better mousetrap. In a term paper he outlined a plan for an express parcel service that would beat a path to everybody else's door.

Later, while flying two hundred combat missions in Vietnam, he refined his concept of an "absolutely, positively overnight" service using the company's own jets, so as not to be tied to passenger schedules, and using a single hub (Memphis) to "keep it simple, stupid" (KISS), which is Smith's motto. He barely got a passing grade on his term paper. But his highly profitable idea has now spawned a bunch of imitators, including the U.S. Postal Service. "People still don't understand the concept," says Smith. "They think we're in transportation. We're really in the package-pipeline business."

The creation of an Evergreen Fund, a Mrs. Fields Cookies, a Mary Kay Cosmetics, or a Federal Express may seem like a single, brilliant stroke. Actually, it is the final stage of a long, slow fermentation process. The result is a distillation of study, experience, and intuition. Intuitive sparks perhaps appear to be thrown off spontaneously. But hovering behind them are usually years of disciplined training.

5

LESSONS FROM THE GRIDIRON AND OTHER FIELDS OF SPORT

THE quick reflexes displayed by professional football players, and more particularly the uncanny play-calling skill of quarterbacks, provide further evidence that preparation—rigorous training and precision drilling in the case of their sport—is a prerequisite of intuition. It's not just the arduous physical conditioning required for blocking and tackling and running and passing that enhances intuition. But many disciplines practiced on the gridiron can hone an intuitive edge useful in other fields, especially in business. Studying these disciplines helps illustrate how intuition can be sharpened with practice.

CONCENTRATION

Concentrating, or calming the mind so it is, in effect, transcended and movement becomes automatic, figures importantly in football's bruising ballet. The most accomplished players claim their peak performances never occur when they are consciously thinking of how to perform. Inspired football, they say, is played with unthinking spontaneity, so that years of experience and training are compressed into split seconds of decision-making.

Champion athletes in other sports tell of a similar mystical feeling that shifts them for fleeting moments to a higher level of perception. Mainly what they describe is increased clarity and the strange sensation of being in total control. They also talk about the stopping of time, describing an "infinite present" with everyone moving in slow motion. "The experience is one of beautiful isolation," wrote Bill Bradley, the former Princeton and New York Knicks star, and now the Democratic senator from New Jersey, in his pro basketball autobiography, *Life on the Run*. "It's as if a lightning bolt strikes, bringing insight into an uncharted area of human experience."

There is evidence that a detached mental state is required for perfect eye-hand coordination. Even duffers know that motor coordination in any sport is badly inhibited by an "analexic" left brain that imposes self-conscious consideration of every body movement, whether it be in a golf swing, swimming stroke, or tennis serve.

To help amateur players overcome this self-defeating self-consciousness, author W. Timothy Gallwey in his brilliant book *The Inner Game of Tennis* uses the concept of Self 1 and Self 2. As he explains his work,

> Self 1 was the name given to the conscious ego mind which likes to tell Self 2, the body and unconscious computerlike mind, how to hit the tennis ball. The key to spontaneous, high-level tennis is resolving the lack of harmony which usually exists between these two selves. This requires the learning of several inner skills, chiefly the art of letting go of self-judgments, letting Self 2 do the hitting, recognizing and trusting the natural learning process, and above all gaining practical experience in the art of concentration.

Gallwey's Self 1 and Self 2 are equivalent to Monitor and Mover, the left and right hemispheres of the brain. Keeping the conscious teller (Monitor) from encroaching on the unconscious, automatic doer (Mover) is as essential in the executive suite as it is on the tennis court or gridiron. "If you had to do everything through thought, choices, and analysis, you wouldn't accomplish much," says Don Rumsfeld, G.D. Searle's former boss, who was captain of Princeton's wrestling team and later all-navy champion. "The skilled executive does eighty-five percent of his work by reflex. That means he can concentrate most of his brainpower and energy on what he doesn't know so well."

Also, the single-track mind that in sports seems to expand time by focusing hard on the present moment—which is crucial to hitting or catching a ball, or pinning an opponent in wrestling—is equally important in business. Adds Rumsfeld: "There are those moments of execution on a job when any distraction that would siphon off just a fraction of your energy can't be tolerated."

Focusing on the future may provide direction and enthusiasm in any competition. But concentrating on the present improves performance. Butterfingered pass receivers are usually thinking about their next move and trying to run with the football instead of concentrating on catching it and locking it securely in their arms. Executives who muff a deal are often eyeing future prospects.

So it appears that the delicate balance between Monitor and Mover may be just as crucial in acing a serve at Wimbledon, blasting a World Series home run, or tossing a Super Bowl touchdown pass as it is in hitting on an exciting new business concept such as the "absolutely, positively overnight" delivery of packages that got Federal Express off the ground. To enhance one's intuitive potential in any field, Monitor must not be given the upper hand.

VISUALIZATION

Former gridiron great Willie Davis grew up dirt-poor in tiny Lisbon, Louisiana. Now he owns one of the biggest beer distributorships in California, a network of five radio stations, part of a company that makes bus shelters, and part of a school supply business. He sits on the boards of Sara Lee, MGM/UA Entertainment, and Fireman's Fund Insurance Companies.

Davis attributes much of his success to intuition. "All my life," he says, "I've had this innate feeling that I was ahead of the whole process. Awareness and anticipation are a hell of an asset."

He also credits three people with helping him a lot: his

mother, Nodie Bell; Secretary of State George Shultz, who was dean of the University of Chicago's business school when Davis got his MBA there in 1968; and his Green Bay Packers coach, Vince Lombardi. With the six-foot three-inch, 265-pound Davis playing defensive end, the Packers won three consecutive National Football League championships. He was all-pro six times and was elected to the Pro Football Hall of Fame in 1980.

Davis recalls that many times he would "actualize" in his mind what he expected to do on Sunday. "It was not unusual," he says, "for me to lie awake at night visualizing exactly how I was going to make it happen, and how the opposing team would attempt to deny my doing it. After the game some of my own teammates would exclaim, 'How in the world did you make that play?' But it was almost as if the play had been made out of this advance perception more than out of ability, like I had gone beyond what I know."

Someday scientists may be able to explain these intuitive occurrences on the playing field. Psychologists and physiologists have conducted numerous experiments over the years in archery, basketball-shooting, dart-throwing, and other games of accuracy to determine the effect of not only visualizing success but trying to mentally experience it as well. Vivid visualization, they conclude, can dramatically improve physical coordination and performance. However, they still don't know why.

The moment of transition from prior visualization to an intuitive flash is reminiscent of Eugen Herrigel's description of the mastery of Japanese ink painting in *Zen in the Art of Archery*. "It is only attained when the hand, exercising perfect control over technique, executes what hovers before the mind's eye at the same moment when the mind begins to form it, without there being a hair's breadth between."

How the hand executes what hovers before the mind's eye depends on the attitude of the beholder. In his book *Golf My Way*, Jack Nicklaus extols the importance of advance mental imagery.

I never hit a shot even in practice without having a very sharp, in-focus picture of it in my head. It's like a color movie. First I see the ball where I want it to finish, nice and white and sitting up high on the bright green grass. Then the scene quickly changes and I see the ball going there: its path, trajectory, and shape, even its behavior on landing. Then there's a sort of fade-out, and the next scene shows me making the kind of swing that will turn the previous images into reality.

But how does this intuitive power, which can so dramatically affect the outcome of a sports contest, translate into physical power? John Brodie, the San Francisco 49ers quarterback for seventeen years and now a football announcer for NBC, claims, "An intention carries a force—a thought connected with an energy that can stretch itself out in a pass play, a golf shot, or in a thirty-foot jump shot in basketball. I've seen it happen too many times to deny it."

Roger Staubach, the former signal-caller who led the Dallas Cowboys for eleven years—and to Super Bowl victories in 1972 and 1978—describes this same phenomenon another way. "There is some kind of mental power in athletics that lets you know you're going to complete a pass or win a particular game," he says. "A lot of it is based on confidence, preparation, and what you put into it." He also found this true in baseball, which he starred in as well as football while attending the U.S. Naval Academy. Now president and sole owner of Staubach Company, a fast-growing Dallas firm that builds, leases, manages, sells, and invests in commercial real estate, he adds: "It's the same in business. I'll get a feeling that something good is going to happen. But that's after I've done everything I can to get ready."

McGill professor Henry Mintzberg's description of the way good managers build mental models of their own business world to help chart future moves sounds very similar to the visualization process professional athletes speak of. But the mental image or model has to be positive, spurred by a feeling, as Staubach says, that something good is going to evolve.

This kind of positive revelation, for example, was experienced by James Rouse, the very upbeat former chairman of the city planning company that still bears his name. A daring developer with a flair for retailing, he created a whole new art form converting dead or decaying downtowns into vibrant shopping and eating oases. "Disciplined harmony" is what he calls the festive conglomeration of stores, food counters, gardens, fountains, lights, and banners that became his trademark. Boston (Faneuil Hall Marketplace), Philadelphia (Gallery at the Market East), Baltimore (Harborplace), and New York (South Street Seaport) have been Roused, so to speak, by his intuitive view of the transformation that was possible.

The mind's eye of a downbeat developer, on the other hand, would have seen only ghosts of the city's past or felt fear of future urban problems. These are intuition's twin blockers. Says Rouse: "People keep asking, 'Why did you continually take such risks?' I didn't regard myself as a risk-taker because I was producing something people have a yearning for. Even in blighted city centers, I felt people yearned for a festival atmosphere." His feeling proved to be right on, and in, the money.

PRACTICE

Roger Staubach also personifies the notion that training and drilling are the two key prerequisites of intuition. "In real estate as in football, it takes a lot of unspectacular preparation to produce spectacular results," he says. Before starting his own company, he put in seven off-seasons in the land syndication division of the Henry S. Miller Company, learning how to play. "There are instincts for funding and closing deals that have to be honed," says the former quarterback, who always considered himself highly skilled in fathoming his opponents' intentions. "You must develop a feeling that there's no way you're going to lose."

Staubach's star receiver on the Cowboys, Billy Joe DuPree, also performed off-season scut work sharpening his business instincts in anticipation of a postfootball career. He began by working for a small Dallas builder pouring concrete foundations and patios. He finally started his own firm because, he says, "there's nothing like having control. It beats running somebody else's plays."

Now as president of DuPree Construction Company, he locates land, obtains financing, and then builds a project with the idea of managing it himself. He is the owner-developer of a $6.5 million, two-hundred-unit apartment complex in South Dallas. "Fighting to get property rezoned is worse than confronting eleven adversaries on a football field," he says. "But I think you'll find football players make the most aggressive businessmen. We don't like to lose," he adds, echoing his former teammate.

As Staubach and DuPree both know, one of the key parts of practice is developing synchronized team play. Of course many former athletes in business have dwelt on the importance of this. The CEO of Phillips Petroleum, C.J. "Pete" Silas, a former basketball star at Georgia Tech, says: "You realize quickly that you can't do it all yourself. If one man is a better shot than the other, they feed him the ball. You play the game around the team you have, just as you adjust to skills in management." Don Rumsfeld, who besides wrestling was also the 150-pound captain of Princeton's football team, says: "Unless you're a Mozart or Einstein most of what you do in life involves working with other people. A lot of this teamwork can be carried out through a sixth sense without even talking."

Practice also teaches poise. This is something Robert Mercer, CEO of Goodyear Tire & Rubber, says he learned playing baseball under Coach Red Rolfe at Yale. "You have to develop poise when you're at the plate facing a pitcher," he points out. After an unsuccessful tryout with the Brooklyn Dodgers in 1947, Mercer wound up playing outfield for Goodyear's industrial team. In 1982 he became boss.

THE WILL TO WIN

The ability of some professional athletes to get psyched up in business as well as in sports seems to be the key ingredient for turning themselves into entrepreneurial stars. But merely wanting to be best in a sport or in any endeavor on any given day falls short of the ultimate goal of improving on human performance. "We know fairly well how to prepare to come close to the limits of performance," writes John Jerome in *The Sweet Spot in Time,* an intriguing book that explores the biophysics of sport. "But to prepare to go beyond them—or to prepare to remain at that stage of readiness at a specific time, for a specific event—requires a level of management that often eludes us."

It's elusive because breaking athletic records, or, for that matter, breaking new ground in science or business, requires a strong intuitive feeling that the feat can be accomplished. As Jerome also points out: "The limits of human performance that we now perceive do not represent physical realities so much as they signify failure of the imagination. Those limits don't really exist; they are ghost images, lying there waiting for us to surpass and dissolve them."

Developer Rouse believes the will to win and to exceed the existing limits of performance is mainly a matter of commitment. Now retired from the Rouse Company, he and his wife, Patricia, founded the nonprofit Enterprise Foundation in Columbia, Maryland, dedicated, as he says, "to seeing that the poor are decently housed within a generation. We are now working in twenty-two cities," he adds, "and hope to be in fifty cities by the end of 1987." To help meet this ambitious goal the Rouses have also launched the Enterprise Development Company, a commercial real estate venture whose profits will flow to the foundation.

To remind himself and others that the battle against urban decay can be won, Rouse carries in his pocket a quotation from Goethe that he frequently hauls out and reads to younger associates:

The moment one definitely commits oneself, then providence moves too. All sorts of things occur to help one that would never otherwise have occurred. A whole stream of events issues from the decision, raising in one's favor all manner of unforeseen incidents and meetings and material assistance which no man could have dreamed would have come his way. Whatever you can do or dream you can, begin it. Boldness has genius, power and magic in it. Begin it now.

Adds Rouse: "All of that I believe down to the bottom of my shoe leather."

TRANSFERABLE SKILLS

The kinship between sports and business skills is demonstrated by the rise of many star athletes to leadership positions in the companies they join. Korn/Ferry International, the executive search firm, surveyed some seventeen hundred senior executives of Fortune 500 companies and found that half of them had played on a varsity team in college. George Munroe, CEO of Phelps Dodge, was a basketball star at Dartmouth and then played a year with the Boston Celtics. IBM's boss, John Akers, played hockey at Yale. Alex Kroll, CEO of Young & Rubicam, was once the star center of the Rutgers football team. David Packard, chairman of Hewlett-Packard, played football at Stanford, as did Manufacturers Hanover's chairman, John McGilli-cuddy, at Princeton. And Mesa Petroleum's boss, T. Boone Pickens, went to Texas A&M on a basketball scholarship. The list goes on and on. But then remember, Ronald Reagan not only played guard for the Eureka College Red Devils but also earned his "E" in track and swimming, while George Bush was Yale's baseball captain.

Star athletes, of course, enjoy celebrity status that gives them an edge when they shift gears and go into business or politics. But their sports skills, too, seem to give them an added advantage. Hidden under Francis Asbury Tarkenton's Minnesota Vikings helmet, it now is clear, was a head naturally attuned to business. "I always considered myself an entrepreneur first and an athlete second," he says. "Making a great play in football gives you an instant jolt. But building a company is a competitive struggle that keeps you on a high."

Back at the University of Georgia, where Fran was a business major, he made the dean's list as well as All-America. In pro ball, he was also a sensation from the start, and the most intuitive, unpredictable player the fans had ever seen. He changed forever the notion that quarterbacks were strong-armed statues standing resolutely in the pocket, ready to pass. Sportswriters used to marvel how well-drilled stalwarts like Johnny Unitas "wouldn't come out of the pocket to meet Raquel Welch." But as Tarkenton points out: "If the rush was on and the pocket collapsed, the play was over." Suddenly, the same sportswriters were marveling how Tarkenton scooted around the field "like he was fleeing from a bank heist." By the time he let fly with the football, they reported, "his pursuers are exhausted and his receivers are somewhere in the next county."

In addition to exclaiming over his "quicksilver feet," reporters also extolled Tarkenton's "agile mind." Not only in the huddle, where as an early exponent of participatory management he would sometimes let linemen call the plays because, as he says, "they were closer to the action than the head coach pacing up and down the sidelines." Off the field as well, Tarkenton inflicted his intuitive ideas on the Vikings' front office, making suggestions about player trades and salaries. But in the end he set records that today's stars are still shooting at: 47,003 yards gained passing, 3,686 completions, and 342 touchdown passes.

There are those who think his eighteen years in the National Football League represent misspent use of a business talent. "Why Fran Tarkenton ever wasted his time in football, I'll never know," says John F. Bergin, president of McCann Erickson, U.S.A. He believes the former quarterback is "an intuitive genius in the art of motivation, who seems to awaken in businessmen a desire to be better managers."

Tarkenton blames business schools for suppressing intu-ition. "They're staffed by profs accustomed to calling all the plays from the sidelines," he says. "In business as in football, if you're punished for trusting your instincts, they'll subside and finally go away."

Today the Tarkenton Productivity Group, a prospering Atlanta-based management consulting company with fifty clients, resurrects the image of an innovative, scampering quarterback—an early-day Doug Flutie—who left some indelible marks on the game. But most of Fran's time is spent huddling with such corporate giants as Boeing, GTE, and Continental Corporation, convincing them to pay his company fees of $50,000 to $250,000 for new efficiency and incentive programs to raise productivity in their offices and plants.

Most consultants sell analyses that drive out intuition. Fran takes a different tack and offers the same kind of insights that he picked up on the playing field: about risk-taking in a corporate structure ("Winning means being unafraid to lose"); about middle managers' need for accu-rate information on how their departments are doing ("Only the boss with a P-and-L knows how the game came out"); and about his pet grievance, the futility of training with no follow-up ("You can't get performance without feedback from the coach").

The transfer of skills from one occupation to another is not limited to athletes who became businessmen. Take the case of Tom Wyman (though he did play soccer at Am-herst), the former CEO of the Minneapolis-based canned food company Jolly Green Giant, who was suddenly up-rooted and repotted as the boss of Black Rock, as the CBS headquarters building in New York City is known in broadcasting circles. He still has no notion why the intuitive but unpredictable CBS founder, William Paley, reached out in 1980 and picked him to preside over the vast communi-cations empire. Perhaps Paley was hiring in his own image, since Wyman was recognized as a highly intuitive leader, even though he had never previously been in broadcasting.

Paying a visit to his seventeen-year-old son at prep

school, Wyman was informed by the boy that he had gone to the school library and found a copy of the CBS annual report. "Dad, CBS has so many businesses and you don't know anything about them," exclaimed Wyman's son. "Don't you think they're going to find out?"

6

FEELING THE PULSE OF THE WORKPLACE

JUST as creativity favors the prepared mind, so does laziness produce lousy hunches. Even the most intuitive CEO, with pronounced right-brain powers, must do his homework to generate educated hunches. And though he doesn't personally crunch the numbers, they better be lurking somewhere in his head while his mind and feet wander into unexplored territory. "There is no resting place for an enterprise or its chief executive in a competitive environment," wrote Alfred Sloan, Jr., General Motors' legendary former chairman, who is recognized as the originator of modern management. A half century ago, Sloan converted the automobile company's old fiefdoms into a coordinated by decentralized organization that survived until the current CEO, Roger Smith, took over and launched another revolution that is still going on.

Homework for the intuitive leader doesn't mean committing to memory a host of facts and figures. As was explained in Chapter 4, thoughts and images stemming strictly from memory can drown out intuition with mental noise. However, moseying around the office, plant, or marketplace and feeling the pulse is an important part of the preparation process for setting off an intuitive spark. Management by Walking Around (MBWA) was the name given this technique by CEOs who know that creative lightning doesn't often strike those who stay closeted inside the executive suite.

Detroit Tigers chairman (and former owner) John Fetzer

says: "Walk through the office and intuition will tell you if things are going well, just as it helps you to read between the lines while sitting at your desk." Fetzer is also a staunch believer in mind over matter—called psychokinesis, or PK, by psychologists. Although he spends time talking with the players, just as he does discussing problems with his other employees in the Fetzer Broadcasting Company, he says that he would never have interfered with the peculiar mannerisms of his former star pitcher Mark Fidrych by suggesting that he stop talking aloud to the baseball and telling it where to go. "People aren't conscious of the tools they use in exercising mind over matter," Fetzer says. "The devices they employ depend on their past experience."

Getting exposure out in the office or plant helps feed intuition in several other ways as well. You see new things, or as former Yankees manager Yogi Berra said, "You can observe a lot by watching." You become aware of what you don't know. Spotting a knowledge gap often stimulates intuition. By exchanging ideas and not keeping problems to yourself, you may also tap into the intuition of others. Even the give-and-take of a bitter business confrontation can set off an intuitive flash. Chief executives love to talk about loneliness at the top. But this is a self-inflicted wound. Self-inhibiting, too, for inducing intuition.

Trammell Crow, the country's biggest real estate developer, who turned downtown Dallas into a shimmering asparagus patch of steel-and-glass skyscrapers, has no office. His desk occupies an open space on the top floor of his new LTV Tower, surrounded by the desks of subordinates. He claims that being in the middle of all the interior traffic "keeps me attuned to what's going on." A onetime CPA, he intended to become a lawyer but got sidetracked during World War II and ended up buying vacant city lots and erecting buildings on them.

"Anybody who tries to make site determinations mathematically, by charts, or by other scientific methods is wrong," he says. "Oddsmaker Jimmy the Greek is right. It's that vast body of experience that you retain in your brain and pull out as you need it that's important in picking winners."

The seventy-year-old Crow speaks slowly and reflectively. At times he wearily rested his forehead on his desk next to my tape recorder, as if his brain waves might transmit directly into the machine. But his words continue audibly: "No man can retain in his consciousness all the things he knows and needs to make a decision. It's just too big a body of knowledge. I believe that business leaders take some positions and make some decisions transcendentally. Not magically. Intuitively."

The most farseeing businessmen, Crow believes, hide their intuitiveness. "The big-deal guys, who act like they're intuitive," he says, "usually hit the wall. Having a receptive mind and heart requires stifling any feeling of being a big shot."

Crow used to meditate ("It's wonderful!"). He also jogged a lot until a surgeon removed the cartilage from his right knee. Now he walks an hour and twenty minutes a day instead. "I do a lot of thinking when I walk," he says. "The daydreaming, Walter Mitty kind of stuff—what I might have done and what I'm going to do." And he takes a pocket Dictaphone along to record those ideas he doesn't want to lose.

REFLECTING FORWARD AND BACKWARD

Management by Walking Around doesn't mean the CEO is absorbing only what he sees, or that the direction he goes in is determined solely by his feet. All during these perambulations, backward and forward reflections are converging in his subconscious mind. This pondering consists partly of analyzing old mistakes, partly in sizing up the chances of future success. John Fetzer calls this "an unconscious weighing of evidence" and reports that he does a lot of the weighing while he's walking around, and that it seems to precipitate some of the decisions he considers to be intuitive.

Wherever it takes place, the review process that precedes

an intuitive flash may be continuous or instantaneous. In either case it's hard to visualize how the process works. Imagine a pair of polished mirrors that are pointed fore and aft, reflecting overlapping images on a single spot inside the brain. The catalyst that eventually turns this mental montage into a bright new vision is the Eureka factor. But before the Eureka factor can function, these forward and backward reflections must be fused with a view of the opportunity that presently exists.

How this all happens depends on the mind's eye of the beholder. Consider Geraldine Stutz, president and managing director of the trendy Manhattan emporium Henri Bendel. She is said to know what people want before they themselves do. When she was hired by Genesco to run the store in 1957, it was a disaster, losing more than $1 million a year on $3 million in sales. "It was everybody's favorite store," she says, "but nobody had been in it for twenty years." Stutz, who was then only thirty-three, had been a fashion model, a fashion-magazine editor, and a shoe-chain manager but had no comparable merchandising experience.

For a few days she just drifted about the almost empty store, sort of shell-shocked. "I had arrived just in time for nobody to come to shop for Christmas," she recalls. "But substrata ideas begin to present themselves when you're wandering around. Out of this meandering I conjured up an image of what the store ought to be." The resurrection started when Stutz unveiled her Street of Shops (the press at first dubbed it the Street of Flops), a jazzy labyrinth of boutiques on the main floor, designed for chic, style-conscious customers. "I never asked myself, 'What do women want?' " Stutz says. "I knew instinctively that I ought to do the kind of store that I would want to shop in. And I had a clear picture of what that store was like—an intimate place with warm, personal service, neither arrogant nor servile, that caters to sophisticated, big-city, small-size individuals who like to wear clothes rather than being worn by them."

By 1962 Bendel was making money, and in 1980 with the backing of a group of Swiss-based investors, Stutz bought the store from Genesco for $8 million. There was no precedent for either transforming the store or taking it over. Gerry, as she's called, admits that it was all done on intuition. "My gift, if I have one," she says, "is picking terrific talent and providing the atmosphere for them to do their best work." But the vision—the boutique concept that has since been copied by many other department stores— came from her nonstop perambulations. As she kept walking around the empty store, her own frustrations as a shopper, combined with the realization of Bendel's dismal sales and missed potential, triggered a clear mental picture of a Street of Shops. Past, present, and future fused into a totally fresh view.

In 1985 The Limited Inc., a large retail chain, bought Bendel with the idea of expanding Gerry Stutz's concept. "There is the potential for Bendels in every major city in the world," claims chairman Leslie Wexner. That prospect excites Gerry, who will stay on as president. "I expect to be involved in everything Bendel does," she says.

SHARPENED SENSITIVITY

While today's CEOs must keep their personal radar sweeping the horizon for unseen hazards, they can't ignore the warning signals from inside their own corporations. More effort is now being put on sharpening internal awareness. In fact, a new mini-industry has sprung up consisting of management consultants who specialize in this. The National Training Laboratory, of Arlington, Virginia, for instance, conducts some 120 workshops a year to coach executives from Fortune 500 companies and government agencies in sensitivity training. Executive Director Joseph Potts says: "Sensitivity is simply intuition about other people. It's not a matter of politeness, but recognizing that feelings inside a business organization are important, and that a company probably won't become creative until the angry parts of its management process are eliminated."

Potts claims that a number of clear lessons usually emerge from these workshops. The participants come away appreciating that: (1) paying attention to their intuition provides added information for executives to work with; (2) other members of the same firm view the world differently than they do, and that these differences are part of a company's creative texture; (3) it pays to stop, look, and listen to reap the benefits of other people's intuition.

A small management consulting firm, Mobley Luciani Associates in New York City, similarly whisks clients away on week-long retreats for sensitivity training to find out where employee attitudes and values are at variance with company views and objectives. "It's a kind of group therapy with bottom-line results," explains Patricia Luciani. "The people who work together are forced to confront each other as individuals. We try to make them go from negative chemistry to positive interaction."

Most frequently what the consulting firm finds gumming up the works is division heads who don't view themselves as team players but as rulers of private fiefdoms, a situation it has discovered to be as rife in nonprofit organizations as it is in profit-making corporations.

Another consulting firm specializing in interpersonal repair work is run by Dr. Paul Mok, a Harvard-trained psychiatrist. Mok began what he calls CST—Communicating Styles Technology—with Drake-Beam Associates in New York. Borrowing heavily from the Swiss psychiatrist Carl Jung, he divided all executives into four types, each characterized by a distinct communicating style.

Intuitor. Wordy but impersonal. Writes in abstract terms. Wears mixed, unpredictable clothing. Likes futuristic office furnishings.

Thinker. Precise and businesslike speech. Writes in well-structured specifics. Dresses conservatively. Prefers a plain, distraction-free workplace.

Feeler. Speech warm and humorous. Writes personalized letters and memos. Clothes are colorful and informal. Adorns office with mementos and snapshots.

Sensor. Abrupt but to the point. Writes brief, urgent notes. Wears functional, unfancy clothes. Too busy to be neat, office often cluttered.

Nobody, Mok points out, is all one type or another. His main effort is concentrated on helping businessmen and women to identify their own communicating style, using a self-administered multiple-choice test about work habits, success expectations, behavior under pressure, and personal deficiencies. He then tries to teach them how to divine the communicating style of the bosses, underlings, and clients they must deal with. "Almost anybody," says Mok, "can adapt to the communicating style of an adversary for short periods of time."

Now in business for himself in Dallas (where he is chairman emeritus of Mok-Bledsoe International and president of Training Associates), he counts Alcoa, Caterpillar Tractor, Exxon, IBM, and Price Waterhouse among his clients. He found that one company he works with suffered from a surplus of thinkers on top. "I urged them to recognize the sensors and feelers in middle management who were being underutilized," he says, adding: "The only trouble is, most companies don't call me until the problem is so acute it may be curtailing sales."

As an example, Mok cites the difficulty that Ross Perot's Electronic Data Systems formerly had signing up banks as clients—until Mok taught the EDS salespeople the gentle art of "style flexing," or getting on the other guy's wavelength. According to Mok, most of the salespeople were super-sensors, while the bankers were largely thinkers. He urged the sales reps to spend more time on their precall planning, slow down their sales pitch, and leave a more detailed presentation for the bankers to mull over. Business improved markedly.

FEEDBACK FROM THE GRAPEVINE

The views of those underlings not on the CEO's wavelength, or not sharing his vision, can also be picked up by listening to the company grapevine. Used intelligently, the grapevine is yet another conduit that can help feed the boss's intuition. But many CEOs regard it as a malicious, morale-sapping influence that conflicts dangerously with the need for secrecy in creating new products and developing new policies—and especially in picking the most competent people for promotion and in firing the nonperformers. An overgrown grapevine, they fear, will turn the premises into a jungle. This fear is felt most strongly by old-fashioned CEOs who still speak of "releasing" information, as if it could be kept from seeping out. However, distrustful CEOs who try to suppress their internal rumor networks should realize that Roman emperors used to send rumor wardens, called *delatores,* out into the street to collect this kind of scuttlebutt because it was useful to them.

It can be useful to the intuitive manager as well, because it provides valuable employee feedback about almost everything going on. A management expert who spent a dozen years studying company grapevines estimates they are 75 percent accurate. They may, in fact, be more reliable than expensive employee opinion surveys conducted by polling organizations. The grapevine—a term that originated with the stringing of vinelike telegraph lines between trees during the Civil War—also performs a number of useful services for employees. It translates formal company orders into their own lingo, spreads information about job performance and employment opportunities, and makes the workplace more close-knit. For those reasons it helps everybody on the premises, including the boss, get on the same wavelength. In addition, it's a great source of entertainment. "Rumors are fun," says William Phillips, chairman of Ogilvy & Mather Worldwide. "It's always nice to know something everybody else doesn't."

What makes rumors so hard to squelch is that they are often shrouded in ambiguity. But for the intuitive manager who wants time to let a new plan of action percolate in his mind before implementing it, the rumor mill may permit a practical arrangement to evolve before the plan is announced. Putting two divisions destined to be merged under one person, or simply giving added responsibility without a change of title to an executive earmarked for promotion, are examples of this. A formal announcement, on the other hand, may freeze the intention into rigidity prematurely.

Japanese managers think that one of the worst afflictions in American business is our penchant for making formal announcements. They believe that most of the actions taken by management will announce themselves, and therefore prefer ambiguity over clarity.

But rumors keep changing as they are relayed, and some of the ambiguity tends to evaporate. In what has long been regarded as the seminal work on the subject, *The Psychology of Rumor* published back in 1947, coauthors Gordon Allport and Leo Postman explain that while the central theme of a rumor may be resistant to change, crucial details keep being deleted, a process they call "leveling." At the same time, the most dramatic details keep being exaggerated ("sharpening"), so that a rumor, like some sort of shrinking missile, keeps getting shorter and more pointed in flight. Therefore, the intuitive CEO must realize that only so much time can be allowed to elapse before a rumor is finally exploded and replaced with an explanation of his real view. Otherwise it may prematurely destroy the idea he is developing.

The national rumor mill generates all kinds of data vital to the intuitive decision-maker. Advance warnings of corporate shake-ups, takeovers, and spin-offs are either leaked intentionally or just seep out. In either case, a defense can often be erected before the event takes place. In our currently volatile economic climate, the global rumor mill likewise produces useful tip-offs about inflation, interest rates, unemployment, and foreign competition. It also spreads the word about international crises with lightning speed.

In business, however, rumors do not fly only in times of crisis and calamity. They are something to be reckoned with every day—and they are not all bad. Ogilvy & Mather's Bill Phillips believes that rumors can change the attitude of a company or an individual and make them more receptive to an idea. "It's amazing, in this business," he says, "how fast feelings change when the agency wins an account. The rumor mill lays the groundwork." Phillips claims that favorable rumors circulating about a new product can lay the groundwork for it as well. "Often the best advertisement is a word-of-mouth endorsement," says the man whose business is developing multimillion-dollar ad campaigns.

But on Madison Avenue, where the grapevine is the established communication link, executives complain that the recent trend to substitute white wine for martinis at lunch has seriously impaired their information-gathering ability. "The grape is shrinking the grapevine," quipped one advertising man.

DANGER VERSUS OPPORTUNITY

Even intuitive businessmen too often miss the opportunity that accompanies a crisis. Jim Rouse, we saw, spotted the opportunity involved in eradicating urban decay from some of our city centers. But he believes that many chief executives are too blinded by a desire for instant profits to give full play to their intuition. They fail to see that discovering a solution to a crisis and earning a profit are often intertwined. But then students of Eastern thought have claimed for centuries that Occidentals are less acute than Orientals in sensing the challenge inherent in a crisis. In fact, there is no Japanese or Chinese word for crisis. The idea is conveyed by two component characters: danger and opportunity.

Danger and opportunity appear at opposite ends of the intuitive decision-maker's spectrum. At the danger end practically all of the computations and permutations can be determined by computer. But opportunity involves incalculable uncertainty. There's no way of spotting new opportunities by computer, though myopic, left-brained managers may think they can. It's been said: "A man with only a hammer perceives a world of nails." The unintuitive manager who expects to spot visions of the future by staring at his computer screen perceives a binary world of bits and bytes. The truly intuitive manager, on the other hand, surveys the whole world around him searching for new clues.

7

WIDE-ANGLE VISION

IT was only a matter of time before fascination with the right-brained boss would spawn a number of books, schools, seminars, and consultants. Inferential Focus in New York City, for instance, has developed a sizable market for "soft information"—gossip, speculation, insights, and other intangibles on which the intuitive mind feeds. The firm furnishes educated hunches ("disciplined intuition" is the term it uses) to some seventy-five clients, including IU International, Chase Manhattan, E.F. Hutton, and the White House Office of Planning and Evaluation.

The idea was simple enough. Since lead time is a precious business advantage, why not collect and sell these seemingly unconnected clues that can sometimes foretell a new economic or social trend? After all, aren't anomalies (events that fall outside expected patterns) often the stuff that hot business hunches are based on? Certainly spotting a market aberration early in the game can enable one company to get the jump on its rivals. And competition is too brisk to sit around waiting to confirm these clues. Because as soon as any new fad, style, or product starts generating numbers, they are instantly cranked into everybody else's computer.

Inferential Focus ferrets out these stray bits and pieces by combining hundreds of publications from *Playboy* to *Iron Age,* from *Soviet Life* to the *Japanese Economic Journal.* When fitted together, the pieces sometimes relay valuable business intelligence, or what this firm, which has been dubbed the CIA for CEOs, calls an "unintended message."

"Key clues are usually picked up in fields far removed from the businesses they affect," says Charles Hess, one of Inferential Focus's three principals. In 1985, for example, his company discerned that champagne sales were up, poker was coming back, and video games were dying—evidence, he says, that baby boomers are essentially homebodies.

But business leaders don't readily grasp the import of such revelations, and their companies naturally resist change. Swiss watchmakers, Hess pointed out, were almost fatally surprised by the advent of the transistor, just as only one out of six American vacuum tube manufacturers many years ago had the foresight to start making transistors. "Anyway," he says, "the pace of change is often too fast for analysis to explain what's taking place." For that reason he tells clients his company would rather be "generally correct than precisely wrong."

Each day the three principals of Inferential Focus pore over news about everything ranging from the weather to social issues and industry developments. Often it is a brief item innocuously ensconced among bigger, more eye-grabbing stories that catches their attention—"a story begging to be overlooked." Once a week Hess and his associates gather to discuss and synthesize the information tidbits unearthed during their solitary scannings. It is from these sessions that early trends are sometimes spotted.

Clients of Inferential pay an average annual fee of $24,000. For this they receive a newsletter every ten days, frequent telephone updates, and a quarterly personal presentation, during which about a dozen "areas of change" are discussed. At these presentations, Hess and his associates try to teach their clients to watch for the unexpected and to question expert opinions. "We emphasize the importance of trusting their own instincts in making decisions," explains Hess. He believes that CEOs in particular must know how to read a lot more than words. They must assimilate gestures and moods and other signals flashed during head-to-head encounters with both colleagues and competitors. In fact, the executive's own language suggests this hunger for sensory information. He wants to get the "big picture," the "feel of the situation," the "hot gossip," and "cold facts." Adds Hess: "This is not what budding young MBAs are taught."

One of the consulting firm's founders, the late Bennett Goodspeed, who held an MBA degree, used to tell clients: "If Thomas Edison had been trained in an MBA program, he would have tried to invent a bigger candle." Shortly before he died, Goodspeed wrote an astute little book titled *The Tao Jones Averages: A Guide to Whole-Brained Investing,* which explains the importance of using intuition in picking stocks. A number of portfolio managers who subscribe to Inferential Focus have recommended the book to their own clients.

Some of the clues on which Inferential Focus bases its "disciplined intuition" are rather esoteric. The return of 17 million birds ("nature's weathermen") to Christmas Island in the Pacific led the company to advise clients that the earth's climate may now be getting back to normal after several years of drought. That bodes well for inflation, Hess believes, because food prices should remain stable.

In recent years, he claims, his company spotted a key clue in 1979 forewarning of gold's steep rise; called the oil price drop in 1980; and concluded in 1983 that estimates of future personal computer sales were euphorically unrealistic. He presently predicts that jogging is peaking. More important to industry, he now surmises that putting robots on assembly lines will standardize future profit margins in manufacturing and shift the money-making opportunities to marketing, where a creative approach can still provide an edge. Says Hess: "We feel that intuition about the marketplace depends a lot on developing this kind of broad vision."

THE ADVANTAGE OF SEEING PERIPHERALLY

Inferential Focus, unlike more traditional forecasting firms that stare straight ahead at the latest economic statistics, puts a high value on peripheral vision. In fact, Hess believes it is one of the strengths of the right-brained boss.

Athletes, of course, have long been aware of the importance of peripheral vision. Quarterbacks rely on it to keep from getting sacked. Hockey and basketball players use it to spot teammates open for a pass and to pounce on their opponents' lapses. Author John McPhee explained in *A Sense of Where You Are*, a book about Bill Bradley's basketball days at Princeton, that his most remarkable gift was his vision. "During a game," wrote McPhee, "Bradley's eyes are always a glaze of panoptic attention, for a basketball player needs to look at everything, focusing on nothing, until the last moment of commitment." McPhee even took the man who is now the Democratic senator from New Jersey to an ophthalmologist to prove that he had an abnormally wide field of vision.

Hess claims that in business as in sports the intuitive players exercise wide-angle vision, spotting new opportunities all over the place, while their less creative counterparts merely concentrate on racking up high profits by focusing narrowly on the bottom line. He cites two of today's superstars, Larry Bird of the Boston Celtics and Wayne Gretzky of the Edmonton Oilers, as highly intuitive models that executives should pay attention to. He even quotes to his clients *Time* magazine's 1985 cover story about the pair: "Their most uncanny power enables them to see and play the game several moves ahead of the moment, comprehending not only where everything is, but also where everything will be." This statement, says Hess, "coincides perfectly with my view of intuition in business."

A unique finishing school for future CEOs in La Jolla, California, that operates remotely by computer tries to inculcate in rising business stars this same ability to view the world peripherally and prophetically. Called the School of Management and Strategic Studies, it is the right-brain child of Richard Farson, cofounder and president of the Western Behavioral Sciences Institute, which started the school in 1982. The course lasts two years, costs $25,000, and features some of the most far-reaching, and far-out, subject matter anywhere. The pupils meet their profs and pick their courses during an indoctrination week at La Jolla. After that they simply tickle the keys of their home computer at night. Instantly school's open—and so, possibly, is a new era in managerial communication.

A computer comes with the tuition. It hooks students up to their professors in a closed-circuit network over which they receive assignments, turn in homework, and can also consult each other on prickly business problems.

The beauty of the system for busy executives is that it's asynchronous, allowing teachers to lecture, students to listen, and discussions to evolve at the convenience of the individual participants. Each student comes on-line whenever he or she wants to, whether early in the morning or in the evening after work. Questions and answers are stored in a central computer (belonging to EIES, or "eyes," as the nationwide Electronic Information Exchange System is known), and the whole educational exchange takes place quietly in ribbons of illuminated print that unroll across each participant's screen. Just in case someone prefers reading black type on white paper, the equipment issued includes a printer that spews out seventy-five lines of print a minute. The school has pulled in pupils from Westinghouse, Digital Equipment, Hewlett-Packard, TRW, and General Mills, as well as attracting a scattering of small entrepreneurs, a college president, a Los Angeles city councilman—even an assistant secretary of commerce.

Unlike advanced management schools at Harvard or Stanford, this one offers no quantitative courses and ignores the sharply focused case study approach. It concentrates, instead, on the humanities and social sciences. As the SMSS catalogue points out, the main objective is to develop a "long view" so executives will "emerge from the two-year program with an ability to balance short-term profitability against long-term viability." To provide this kind of vision, Farson has signed on professors with diverse specialties: philosophers, anthropologists, futurists (Herman Kahn was one of the profs until he died), even a climatologist. But they are all lofty thinkers who don't always relate to the bottom-line problems of business.

Each six-month semester begins with another weeklong seminar in La Jolla. One fringe benefit of this management school is being summoned to an idyllic seashore resort where whales frolic in clear view on the horizon. But the tightly scheduled indoctrination sessions running from 9 A.M. until 10 P.M. are no vacation. Mornings consist of small discussion groups at which the students meet professors they will work with on-line after everybody returns home. Evenings are devoted to buffet dinners and general lectures.

The students each select one major, or "main project conference," for study during the semester. Some of these are pretty far-out. For example, students might choose between Climate and Society (the effects of big outbursts of unusual weather on the economy), taught by Walter Orr Roberts, holder of nine honorary degrees and now professor of astrogeophysics at the University of Colorado; and Cultural Resources: The Invention of Benign Genres, given by Stewart Brand, creator of the *Whole Earth Catalog*. (He defines benign genres as "proliferating instruments that do no harm," such as Gandhi's nonviolent disobedience, aerobic exercises, and credit cards—"all elements," Brand adds, "of a resilient society.")

Additionally, the students select two minors, or "parallel conferences." One of these was recently given by psychologist Alex Bavelas, a former Stanford professor who was introduced as a "master at demythologizing business," exploding such myths as "the more information an executive has, the better the decision will be."

Some students, as did Robert Greber, president of Lucasfilm Ltd., feel a little apprehensive when they enter the program. "At first I thought I'd been ripped off," he says. This same kind of criticism has been expressed by others upon discovering that the school gives no exams, grades, or, for that matter, degree. Nevertheless, the School of Management and Strategic Studies avoids the most frequent criticism leveled against other executive education programs. This Computer U, as it has been called, requires no prolonged absence from work and causes no prickly reentry problems when it is time to go back.

More important, Dick Farson, who doubles as dean and chief recruiter for the school, believes that the SMSS curriculum is more appropriate for today's business environment. He contends that corporate leaders presently face too much complexity and turbulence to rely on old quantitative solutions. "They must look at things as interconnected systems rather than in terms of cause and effect," he says. "But by the time they become chief executives they can't spare the hours needed to get on a computer at home each day and study that kind of interpretive thinking." Adds Farson: "Management is getting harder all the time. It's become impossible for an executive to describe what it is that he or she brings to the job. An acceptable shorthand definition is intuition, which is really another term for a huge experience bank."

A WHOLE BRAIN CATALOGUE

Ned Herrmann, chairman of the Whole Brain Corporation in Lake Lure, North Carolina, claims he can winnow out executives with the kind of perception Farson is talking about. Herrmann has concluded that CEOs can manage better by first determining if their subordinates have predominantly left- or right-hemisphere skills. So he devised a 120-question survey called a brain-dominance profile to find out which is which. An executive who winds up in a job for which his brain ill suits him, Herrmann reasons, will probably be miserable. In fact, many alcoholics, he claims, are right-brainers struggling in left-brain slots. Founded in 1983, Whole Brain now earns better than $2 million a year selling this concept to business.

"People used to think the brain was not an appropriate subject to be discussed on company property," says Herrmann. "And would you please knock it off during lunch." Today he claims the subject is very much in vogue at many large corporations such as GM, GE, IBM, and Shell, all of which are his clients.

But Herrmann is no longer satisfied with the simple, unsophisticated left-brain and right-brain dichotomy. He views the hemispheres as being subdivided into limbic and cerebral quadrants, each representing a specialized mode of thinking. Cerebral left he describes as "rational, cognitive, and quantitative, dealing basically with facts." Limbic left is "organized, sequential, and procedural, dealing mostly with structure and controls." The cerebral right quadrant, he says, "is visual, conceptual, and simultaneous, and can be thought of as open in contrast to controlled." On the other hand, the limbic right is "emotional, expressive, and interpersonal, and can be thought of as feelings rather than facts."

One of Dr. Roger Sperry's collaborators, who helped uncover the right- and left-brain specialties, is highly skeptical of Herrmann's claims. "I've gotten so sick of people making piles of money on data that never came out of the lab," Jerre Levy told *Discover* magazine. But Herrmann is convinced of his own findings. "As I looked at the incoming data from the surveys," he says, "there would be the technical, engineering types in cerebral left: administrative, bookkeeper types in limbic left; personnel-oriented, humanistic people in limbic right; and innovators, entrepreneurs, and visionaries in cerebral right."

Herrmann admits that he spent his early years "responding to urges that came from opposite sides of my brain." As a child he loved both math and art. At Cornell he took a curious double major in physics and music. "I came at this as an artist searching for the nature and source of creativity," he says.

Later, as chief of manager education at General Electric, he simultaneously headed the Stamford, Connecticut, Art Association. But in 1983 he left GE to found the Whole Brain Corporation, which now has some thirty employees divided between Lake Lure and Cambridge, Massachusetts. More than 100,000 business people have already submitted to Herrmann's brain-dominance survey, which he refers to as "the instrument." Thousands more have attended his seminars on brain specialization or received his private counseling. However, those who make the best chief executives, he believes, use the two sides of their brain equally. "The CEO who's confined to one mode of thinking can't hack it," he says.

A number of other right-brain proponents have made inroads in American business, and done a little business for themselves along the way. Professor Weston Agor, director of the masters of public administration program at the University of Texas at El Paso, and president of a consulting firm called ENFP Enterprises, puts on daylong seminars for company and government officials. He stresses the importance of taking brain dominance into account in hiring, firing, promoting, assigning work, and in forming committees. His textbook *Intuitive Management: Integrating Left and Right Brain Management Skills* is now used by a number of universities.

Betty Edwards, a California teacher and author of the book *Drawing on the Right Side of the Brain,* exhorts her students to suppress the verbal left hemisphere, and to rely on the artistic right in learning to sketch. One way to do this, she advises, is to sketch things upside down. The idea is to make it more difficult for the logical left brain to recognize the subject matter. That way, Edwards says, the right brain is free to draw what it really sees rather than what it ought to see. Her book more broadly presents a set of basic exercises designed to release creative potential and deepen artistic perceptions.

Another book intended to teach right-hemisphere methods is Marilee Zdenek's *The Right Brain Experience*. It advises readers to free their minds of left-hemisphere inhibitions by studying mandalas (symmetrical designs based on Oriental symbols for the universe), writing with their nondominant hand, and recording dreams.

All this right-brain exploitation has stirred a reaction from the scientific community. Sally Springer, a psychologist at the State University of New York at Stony Brook and coauthor of *Left Brain, Right Brain,* also complained to

Discover that "the evidence we have now is that both hemispheres get involved in virtually everything we do. That doesn't mean these management experts aren't on to something. But to say that it works because of differential use of the two hemispheres goes well beyond what we can prove today."

On the other hand, business's fascination with the subject is understandable. At a time of economic turbulence, when many American companies are under siege at home and abroad, it's very appealing to hear experts say, "We've got a concept backed by the latest neurological discoveries that can help you whip your competitors."

But the fact is, intuitive powers are highly subjective and can't be tested with a simple questionnaire or turned on and off by a seminar. The intuitive process consists of allowing ideas buried deep inside the unconscious mind to slip to the surface, and that can't be done by conscious effort. As soon as we reflect, deliberate, or conceptualize, unconsciousness is lost. Thought interferes. Admittedly, far more environmental information seeps into our subconscious than we suspect. But there is a barrier between conscious and subconscious, a vital filter that protects us from being swamped by sensations, teachings, or self-doubts. The intuitive mind needs time to itself, time to let subterranean ideas percolate and incubate, if the Eureka factor is going to work. This incubation process is covered in the next part of the book.

III
INCUBATION

8

OPENING A PATH

THE brain contains its own guidance system. It shuts out all but specifically selected information. It turns down the brilliance of the day, automatically tunes out distracting sounds in the environment that do not suit its needs, and opens what Aldous Huxley called the "doors of perception." The mind focuses itself on the problems at hand, not on extraneous matters. A man who is hungry does not hear the leaves rustling, it is said. An executive concentrating on a problem does not necessarily hear the voices of superiors or subordinates vying for his attention. Unmonitored, his mind may hear its own inner voice speaking from deep down inside.

Dr. Eugene Gendlin, a University of Chicago psychology professor and author of the book *Focusing,* is experimenting with executives and other human guinea pigs, attempting to induce intuition. He also offers Focusing for Decision-making workshops to corporate leaders interested in learning his technique. "You can train people so they have the capacity to get a hunch anytime they want one," he claims.

This, he says, involves two steps: first, heeding certain body sensations to feel how an idea sits physically; and second, even if the idea produces an uneasy feeling, focusing on it further for a minute or two. "Then," claims Gendlin, "the ideas will usually open up so you find out what's causing the agitation." You may discover that the discomfort is irrelevant and the idea good enough to go ahead with. Or if the ill-at-ease sensation persists, you may find it stems from certain factors that you originally overlooked. In that case you'll probably come up with a better idea, he predicts.

What triggers these bodily reactions? "The executive's accumulated experience," Gendlin says. And where does one look for these telltale body signals? "In the stomach and chest." But he also warns that it takes being able to sit still for a minute or two, concentrating on one topic. "That isn't easy for high-powered executives to do," he says.

Whether or not intuition can actually be induced upon demand, a process can be initiated that may spur it into action. "How do you write a novel?" I asked James Jones some thirty years ago, after he had finished *From Here to Eternity*. "It's simple," he said. "You write one page every day, and at the end of a year you have three hundred and sixty-five pages." Businessmen and women can employ the same simple strategy: start and don't stop until you've created what you want, perhaps much more than you set out to.

In other words, grab one corner of a problem and begin to unravel it, and the solution may manifest itself before you've gone very far. "Action without attachment to the fruits of the action" is how taking this path is described in Karma Yoga. The word "yoga," in fact, mean "path," and as Yoga scholar Ramamurthi said: "All paths converge toward the ultimate goal." So it may matter little precisely where you begin.

In any case, you can't make the subconscious mind stick to a schedule or conform to the deadline of a business. While focusing, the mind must also be given freedom for ideas to float in and out. Direct assaults on a problem or on a new idea often fail to produce results—or worse yet, cause enough aggravation to smother the intuitive process. Isn't straining to remember a name almost a sure way of not being able to recall it? Relaxing, on the other hand, and letting the mind wander off in another direction, gives it freedom to find the answer.

Some entrepreneurs quite similarly keep floating in and

out of new ventures guided entirely by their gut feelings. And very successfully, too. Frank Crerie, chairman of the Stan West Mining Corporation in Phoenix, is on his fourth entrepreneurial incarnation. During the early atomic days when everybody was chasing uranium, he founded what is now called Standard Metals. Not satisfied with his success, he formed a second uranium mining company called Stan Rock. Still restless, he organized White Shield, an oil exploration company, which made the first strike in the Aegean Sea and then branched out into Southeast Asia, obtaining highly profitable concessions in Indonesia. Its stock, issued at $1, split and resplit, hitting $30 before Crerie became restless once again and pulled out. But by this time he was a millionaire many times over. "What's fun," he says, "is getting an idea, perhaps an intangible dream, and then making that dream happen. But once it does I kind of lose interest."

Crerie's dream today is to reactivate the old McCabe gold mine in the foothills of the Bradshaw Mountains near Prescott, Arizona. A hundred years ago, five thousand miners using steam-powered drills and dynamite rapidly exhausted its veins. But by probing deep under the defunct shafts with modern equipment, Crerie and his partner, geologist Stanley Holmes, discovered untouched rich lodes containing at least five years' worth of proven ore. Prospects were sufficiently bright to entice a subsidiary of Sante Fe Southern Pacific to invest $15 million and enter into a joint operating agreement with Crerie's company. "This whole venture is sort of a happy accident," he says. "I was never a gold bug before. But when you can produce a hundred thousand ounces of gold a year for less than two hundred dollars an ounce, it turns you into one."

In the same way, important scientific discoveries have been made accidentally by taking an unexpected detour off a well-trodden path. Scottish bacteriologist Alexander Fleming noticed that some of the colonies of bacteria he had been cultivating died because the petri dishes containing them had become contaminated. Quite logically, he might have tossed out those dishes and started anew. Instead,

Fleming sensed something significant and by pursuing his hunch discovered penicillin.

A ROAD THAT'S ALWAYS SLIPPERY

How, then, does one pursue the most likely paths leading to intuition? There is no sure route, but there are a number of recommended procedures that may help nudge you in the right direction: (1) Keep the overall problem continuously in mind. (2) Redefine the problem frequently. (3) Consider many alternatives simultaneously. (4) Don't be afraid of maintaining an unsophisticated, childlike view. As Picasso said, "It takes a long time to grow young." (5) Pursue trial and error thinking, but rely on nonverbal imagery. The intuitive French mathematician Henri Poincaré described lying in bed imagining clouds colliding and combining as the basis of his discovery of the Fuchsian functions. (6) Distinguish between real obstacles and imagined ones that don't have to be surmounted. (7) Don't feel compelled to excuse a zigzag or obscure route to an objective. The right path is hard to discern. (8) Don't count on instant success. Feel confident of being able to absorb a string of setbacks en route to an elusive goal. The road to intuition, after all, is always slippery.

There are certain physical surroundings and activities that are conducive to intuition. Lying on a beach or peacefully contemplating the countryside from a mountaintop may still the mind and make it more perceptive. Jogging can, too; it also improves circulation and provides the brain with biochemical nutrients, especially glycogen, an energy-rich carbohydrate. Meditation is known to induce a relaxed alpha state (a rhythm of 8 to 12 brain-wave cycles per second) or theta state (characterized by the slower and slower brain waves—4 to 7 cycles—preceding sleep).

Experiments have shown that the more meditative experience a Zen monk has, the more theta he can generate. Even in the depths of theta, a Zen master is not asleep but mentally alert and experiencing a strong feeling of well-being. It is during this state that sudden realizations spring

intuitively from his unconscious. Biofeedback experts trying to teach their patients to heal themselves by emulating
the monk's feeling of physical regeneration while meditat-
ing have trouble keeping their patients awake in the theta
state. The patients tend to slip off into the delta state (0.5 to
4 cycles) of sleep.

During its normal waking beta state (13 to 30 cycles), the
mind jumps from thought to thought, causing a jerky
brainwave pattern. The alpha and theta patterns are tranquil
and prime the mind to be more perceptive. For this reason
a few corporations have set aside short periods of quiet time
each day when every manager from executives down to
foremen on the assembly line can gather their thoughts.

Meditation is not intended to trigger thoughts of any
kind. It simply reduces tension and anxiety, which hamper
intuition. Fasting may further quiet the mind, sometimes
producing a "raised state"—the deepest form of concentration, which the Buddhists call *samadhi*. At the same time,
stress, pain, exhaustion, and boredom have the opposite
effect, agitating the mind and blocking the pathways to
intuition.

MIND-SET OF A RECEPTIVE STATE

For executives interested in making creative decisions,
achieving a receptive state of mind is more important than
understanding the various rhythms of brain waves inside
their head. To open an intuitive path requires openness and
faith, a belief that whatever route is taken won't turn out to
be a blind alley. Oriental mystics have traditionally smiled
inscrutably and said: "We are limited only because we
believe we are limited."

Another important requirement for the Eureka factor to
work is the readiness to believe that a flash of inspiration
may indeed come at any moment. People in such a receptive
state have sometimes described themselves as feeling
"light-bodied." They are also occasionally observed tilting
their head slightly to the right, as if favoring that brain
hemisphere.

All of these sensations and appearances aside, psychologists state emphatically that memories and ideas are constantly being arranged below the conscious level of the brain, which sorts and interprets them into a final impression. It is the so-called semantic memory that sorts out the meanings and knowledge pertinent to your current mental activity.

The resulting impression may be extremely positive, coaxing you down a path to a desired goal. In *Psycho-Cybernetics*, author Dr. Maxwell Maltz wrote: "You must learn to trust your creative mechanism to do its work and not jam it by becoming too concerned or too anxious as to whether it will work or not, or by attempting to force it by too much conscious effort. You must let it work, rather than make it work." Dr. Jonas Salk, discoverer of the polio vaccine, expresses the same idea more simply. "Intuition will tell the thinking mind where to look next," he says.

Trust, therefore, is crucial to opening a path to intuition. You must have faith that it will work. Nobel Prize winner Niels Bohr was once observed nailing a horseshoe to his back door. "Why are you doing that?" asked a neighbor. "For good luck," answered Bohr. "But surely you don't believe it works," protested the neighbor. "True enough," said Bohr. "But I understand it works whether I believe it or not."

Many business leaders exhibit this kind of blind faith in keeping a channel open to whatever it is that sparks their creativity. The intuitive Tisch brothers, Laurence and Preston, chairman and president of the Loews Corporation, have bought their hotels, real estate, and other companies (CNA Insurance, Lorillard Corporation, and Bulova Watch) not in accordance with any master plan, but in response to whatever came along that felt just right to them. "Loews doesn't have a mergers and acquisition department or a planning department," explains Jim Tisch, vice president of financial analysis and one of Larry's sons. "The company doesn't have a bureaucracy in place to figure out what to do. It seizes opportunities."

Seizing opportunities that "feel right" is the self-proclaimed specialty of Steven Greenberg. It enabled him to amass a fortune estimated at $50 million before he was forty. Greenberg, whose prematurely white shoulder-length hair evokes memories of Ben Franklin (another great opportunity-seizer when lightning struck), is chairman of a one-man New York investment relations company called Anametrics Inc. His mirrored penthouse office, filled with Art Deco treasures, sits atop the Rainbow Grill in New York's Rockefeller Center. "Empathy," says Greenberg, "opens up a path to other people's minds. It enables you to read their thoughts correctly, which is the key to intuition." But, he adds, "that's something you can't learn."

Greenberg claims this ability enables him to "read people over the phone. I can tell if they're stiff or loose," he says. "And I can hear it in their voice if they're smiling." He encourages clients to call him anytime. "Call me at four A.M. if you want," he tells them. "When I'm asleep my phone's shut off." Greenberg practically eats and sleeps with a telephone tucked against his ear under his long white tresses. But then his fees for all this conversing range from $10,000 to $200,000 a month.

As a consultant to the CEOs of several successful companies, including Commodore International, Bally Manufacturing, and Wendy's, Greenberg has always insisted on receiving equity as well as a fee. He gets this mainly for making good judgment calls that help to bolster his clients' stock. "Most people sense instinctively when things are wrong," he says. "Or at least they have twenty-twenty hindsight about their mistakes. I sense when things are right."

For an entrepreneur to sense that something is right can take awhile. Ingenious ideas are like flowers. They do not sprout from the soil of the subconscious in full bloom. So let the first tender shoots take shape before trying to consciously grasp what they are. Playing with the idea prematurely may prevent it from budding. Temporary neglect, on the other hand, may result in a spurt of growth. Either way, the maturation process of an intuitive thought is probably out of its originator's control. Nobody appreciates this more than the young inventor or entrepreneur who is trying to plant out in the marketplace the seeds of an idea forming inside his head.

To assist in just this sort of seeding, a new "first-round" venture capital fund was organized recently in Palo Alto, California. Called ONSET, it has as its announced purpose to "bring bright ideas out of the realm of imagination and into a new high-technology company." But what separates ONSET from other seed funds is a requirement that one of its partners become totally committed to the raw idea and volunteer to join the innovator's team. So ultimate success depends not only on the inventor's intuition but on the venture capitalist's intuition as well.

"We probably have concocted the most extreme form of personal punishment for intuition there is," says Terry Opdendyk, one of ONSET's general partners. "We have to go in and run these embryonic companies and make them successful." That, he claims, means saying: " 'I'm emotionally committed to this project and will throw my body in the way of any obstacle for at least one year.' That's quite a responsibility when there's no management team or business plan to start with. Only the kernel of an idea."

Opdendyk points out, too, that the innovative process is often incompatible with the execution process. "So the time comes when the investor has to put constructive blinders on the innovator. Extraneous ideas have to be shunted aside, and a firm focus kept on what's going on. Also, there has to be a sense of where the risks are and how to avoid them. Otherwise, intuition leads nowhere."

OPENING ORIGINAL THOUGHT PATHS
IN GIANT CORPORATIONS

In large publicly owned corporations the problem is almost reversed. Instead of blinders, binoculars are needed to encourage farseeing and intuitive thinking. Irving Shapiro recognized this need when he was named chief executive of Du Pont. Although he has since gone back to lawyering, he was picked by Du Pont for managerial skills that enabled him to effectively coordinate a business empire so vast that it creates its own values—"Values," he admits, "which may be wrong."

Shapiro wanted people around him, therefore, who did not necessarily reflect his view. He warned that too agreeable a personal chemistry at the top of a company can produce an incestuous intellectual atmosphere. "Whoever sits in the CEO's chair is fallible," he says. "When mistakes happen it's because people who knew better didn't speak up."

Professor Eugene Jennings of the Michigan State University Business School has long emphasized the importance of opening conduits for creative thinking in big corporations. He, too, warns of the danger of an incestuous relationship at the top, the kind that often exists between chief executive officers and chief operating officers. "Two heads are not better than one," he says, "unless they work independently. I've seen two people, with this incredible bond between them, just about destroy a company to maintain their own relationship."

Close personal relationships all the way down an enterprise can hobble creativity. Edwin Land, founder of Polaroid Corporation, warned years ago that "there is no such thing as group originality, group creativity, or group perspicacity," even though, he pointed out, "there is something warm and cozy about this picture of the human race marching forward, locked arm in arm and mind to mind."

Polaroid continued for many years to keep the giant Eastman Kodak at bay in the development of the instant camera, accomplishing this feat by stressing individual thought. "Profundity and originality are attributes of single, if not singular, minds," Land advised not long after forming his corporation. He further pointed out that "science is not a river that anyone can sail on."

He might have also added that it takes strong-willed, single-purpose rowers as well. But more than anything, it takes an intuitive navigator not to get sidetracked in some swampy bayou of indecision along the way to the clear, cool headwaters where invention originates.

9

AVOIDING ANALYSIS PARALYSIS

CONSTANTLY accumulating new information and numbers, without giving the mind a chance to percolate and come to a conclusion intuitively, can delay any important decision until the time for action expires. This immobility, caused by substituting study for courage, has been labeled analysis paralysis. The problem might also be called the intuition-avoidance dilemma. But by any name, it represents an example of Monitor's gaining supremacy over Mover in management brains.

Blind confidence in the computer, of course, exacerbates analysis paralysis. Data addicts sit worshipfully before their CRTs waiting for answers to appear. And the addiction will certainly worsen as the new generation of computers possessing "artificial intelligence" comes into play.

These Orwellian thinking machines not only solve problems algorithmically—by the numbers, that is—but also by processing the words and symbols used in such specialized jobs as evaluating casualty insurance risks or assaying hidden dangers in genetic engineering. Promises of still more intelligent computer programs, some even possessing judgmental skills, cannot be dismissed as idle engineering chatter. But whatever develops in the way of expanded electronic wizardry is bound to extend the human intuition-avoidance problem.

"You can get miles and miles of printout data," says Edgar Bronfman, Seagram's CEO. "You can buy packages and programs that will tell you in statistical terms every-

thing you ever wanted to know about anything and maybe
had the good sense not to ask. And while you're studying
the passing parade of data, you may very well fail to hear
the sound of opportunity knocking."

THE CONSULTANT'S LEXICON OF ILLS

Undermining business's trust in intuition is its heavy
dependence on management consultants. Most consultants,
of course, have nothing to sell but the analytic approach.
They are trained to break down jobs into carefully analyzed
components, a process that automatically drives out intuition. Above all, they create order and structure, both
enemies of creative thinking. PERT (Program Evaluation
Review Techniques) and MBO (Management by Objective)
are the call letters of these purveyors of business logic. And
they broadcast them everywhere in the hope of drumming
up more clients.

On the surface the consultant's brand of analysis has
certain advantages over using intuition in problem-solving.
For one thing, executives can be trained in it, which is why
graduate schools of business administration, those ivied
halls of analysis paralysis, prosper and proliferate, and why
the case study method is so popular in their classrooms.

A misguided notion also exists in business today that
analysis is the cheapest way to solve a problem. It does
represent a low initial investment. But the operating cost of
constantly gathering additional information to be analyzed
is high. Just the reverse is true of intuition. The initial
investment in knowledge and experience is steep, while the
operating cost of tapping into this subconscious information
storehouse is virtually nil.

In defense of consultants, it should be pointed out that
their concepts are aimed at expanding time and providing
peace of mind, thus enabling a boss and his subordinates to
be more contemplative and intuitive. The only trouble is
that these hired guns, who are called in to improve
decision-making procedures and to eradicate analysis paralysis, frequently compound the problem by overanalyzing it

as well, all the while expounding on a host of related ills: Procrastination Quotients (a high PQ indicates a tendency to dally on tough decisions); Stacked Desk Syndrome (enables an executive to say to himself, "Look how busy I am"); Open Door Myth (invites interruptions); Planning Paradox (failure to plan because it takes time); and Fat Paper Philosophy (induced by memo-itis and spread by copiers and word processors).

While hopping hither and yon attacking these supposedly dread diseases, the left-brained consultants never advocate putting just a little more reliance on good old gut feelings. That wouldn't conform to their analytic approach. Instead, each one offers a different prescription for helping the harried executive get better organized.

Tight control of meetings in terms of both time and agenda is generally recommended, but with variations. One expert advises using a Danish device called an Econometer that ticks away, revealing the rapidly rising costs of a meeting as computed from the hourly pay of those present. Another suggests stand-up meetings because they break up faster. Still another prescribes preventive measures against something called reverse delegation in chance meetings, citing the example of a boss passing a subordinate in the office corridor:

"Good morning," says the subordinate. "By the way, Boss, we've got a problem." As the consultant explains, the boss knows enough to get involved but not enough to make an on-the-spot decision.

"So glad you brought that up," responds the boss politely. Right away the monkey has been transferred from the subordinate's back to the boss's back.

The care and feeding of monkeys, warns this consultant, is one of the biggest time-killers in business. His recommendation: "Avoid becoming your subordinate's subordinate." The consultant, however, makes no mention of using a little intuition: Steer clear of subordinates with problems, or cut them off by saying, "I'm sure you can solve it" if they begin unloading those problems on you.

REVOKING PARKINSON'S LAW AND
THE PARETO PRINCIPLE

Whatever it costs the business community, analysis paralysis is deemed by some executives to be inescapable. A couple of widely accepted axioms make the frittering away of valuable executive time seem an integral part of the modern corporation. The often-quoted Parkinson's Law, for example, states that "work expands so as to fill the time available for its completion." A good part of that expandable work consists of reviewing and analyzing information about things that have already happened.

From the Pareto Principle (named after economist Vilfredo Pareto, who discovered in the late nineteenth century that 20 percent of the people in Italy controlled 80 percent of the wealth) evolved the so-called 80/20 Rule. According to this, it has been computed that the most trivial 20 percent of an executive's accomplishment consumes 80 percent of his time, while the most vital 80 percent of what he does receives only 20 percent of his attention. However, as is true of most analyses, not much remedial action has resulted. So the question remains: How can cold-eyed captains of industry, who are constantly analyzing return on investment, permit such a paltry return on their own time?

A few perceptive business leaders have implemented protective measures, revoking Parkinson's Law and the Pareto Principle. Steven Greenberg, the Anametrics Inc. chairman, advises: "Without being disrespectful, tell people right away there are certain things you aren't interested in." He also says: "Don't dillydally around. Make decisions in a hurry about what you do want to do."

Greenberg says he has always been a quick study. While he was still at the New York University Graduate School of Business he spotted a truck bearing an attractive logo: "Office Canteens." He jotted down the telephone number. "It's the only time I've ever bothered to record a telephone number painted on the side of a truck," he says. "Three months later another student and I, with the help of some other investors, acquired the company. We sold it a couple of years ago. But not until it became the biggest food service operator in New York City."

Working for his clients occupies a large part of Greenberg's time, but it accounts for only a fraction of his income. Most of his wealth comes from personal investments, some in the "fun" category, like the roller rink he built in New York City. "I play," he explains, "by making spur-of-the-moment deals that I know are going to work." One of his best is Edgecomb Steel, the largest steel service center operating in the United States, with annual revenues of more than $600 million. Greenberg put the company together in about a year. In 1984 it was the number-one performing NASDAQ Over-the-Counter stock.

As might be surmised, Greenberg does not suffer from analysis paralysis. "Lawyers do," he says. "As a group they are the most intelligent entrepreneurs in the country. Too intelligent," he adds. "They can always find a reason for not doing a particular deal." That's why lawyers don't start outside businesses, he claims. "They will serve as advisers or become investors. But they never take that intuitive leap themselves."

Continental Airlines chairman Frank Lorenzo is another action-oriented CEO with no patience for the perpetual reviews and reevaluations his industry is famous for. He sensed the implications of deregulation long before most of his competitors. And he positioned Continental to take advantage of the coming freedom. "It's not enough to have a vision of the future," he says. "You must also insist on your business operating in accordance with that view."

Lorenzo happens to be one Harvard Business School grad who harbors a deep distrust of most think tank-type analysis. "Except," he says, "as it aids and strengthens your sixth sense. If you wait around for the analysis to be completed—to get even eighty percent of the facts—opportunity has passed you by."

Worse yet, he claims, the conclusions drawn from extended analysis are often wrong. "In our business," he says, "analysis will say you should go left when instinct says go right. We find that all the time in fare-structuring. Analysis tells us to raise fares. Our intuition tells us no, we shouldn't. We should keep pressure on the marketplace and do things out there that are very vivid to the consumer."

Even so, the fear of triggering fare wars has been one of Lorenzo's biggest concerns. While a lot of gut feeling goes into that part of Continental's decision-making, Lorenzo warns his sales and marketing people: "Always remember the other guy's got to make a buck too. If you don't leave him a profitable option, you'll hit his hot button." For this reason he calls price-setting in any business an intuitive art form. "I'm surprised," he says, "how many people think you can throw a hand grenade at a competitor and expect he'll stand there and enjoy it."

Allen Neuharth's decision to launch *USA Today*, and in effect throw a hand grenade at local newspapers clear across the country, seemed logical enough in terms of the Gannett Company's desire to get a better return on certain under-utilized assets. Its printing plants in thirty-eight states were operating only a few hours a day. Some eighty separate reportorial staffs were pounding out many more stories than made it into print. And Neuharth saw that satellite transmission could merge all this into a network for producing a national paper.

The unanswered question, Neuharth told *Fortune*, "was whether there was a market for this kind of a project." He and his staff plowed through mountains of market research seeking the answer. Some forty thousand households had delivered a somewhat hazy message: Maybe. His decision, however, was: Go! After three years and $350 million in pretax losses, the answer is still: Maybe. Neuharth indicates that the move wasn't based on logic alone. "Quite a number of us in Gannett," he says, "were still fairly young and aggressive and hungry."

With an intuitive leader like Neuharth, the hunger for success can move a mountain of research. But then most CEOs have the clout to make an intuitive call, especially when the research is murky. Besides, creative bosses appreciate that any kind of market research covers only half of the human responses, those which can be quantified and run through a computer. "I've never been surprised by research," says Bruce Gray, president of R.R. Bowker, which owns *Publishers Weekly* and operates an electronic data service about the book business. "Research is more of a confirmation tool than a discovery tool."

Rance Crain, president of Crain Communications, which publishes *Advertising Age* and twenty-four other business and hospital journals, is even less committed to statistical research. "It makes me nervous and impatient analyzing things by numbers," he says. "They don't shed much light on reality." Rance, who serves as the company's editorial director (his mother, Gertrude Crain, is chairman and CEO), admits that he is guided more by a combination of talking to people and by his own instincts. When *Ad Age* switched from its traditional weekly frequency to twice a week in 1985, the decision was based entirely on personal interviews with executives in the advertising business. "I would have worried if the research didn't confirm what they told us."

Creative bosses like Crain are also instinctive integrators. They have a penchant for putting things together, not chopping them up, which is the function of analysis. Bureaucracies are very analytic, it is said. They demand rational, explicit arguments. Intuition, however, is bureaucracy's fifth column. It undermines the established order and structure.

All of this is not to say there is no room for analysis in business. But just as analysis can be used to buttress intuition, so can intuition be used to punch holes in analysis. A CEO is entitled to feel uneasy with a financial forecast of a future he viscerally feels is not going to happen. "The accountants in general have the upper hand," says William Andres, former chairman of Dayton-Hudson Corporation. "Their analysis is more precise. You have to personally weigh in to support the softer case."

Business psychologists recommend a few easy moves to counter the weight of analysis: (1) Use imagination to offset the tendency to be rational. (2) Get accustomed to proceeding with an incomplete picture. (3) Look for relationships between diverse problems. Solving one helps to solve another. (4) Initiate simple rules of thumb (heuristics) that can bypass analysis.

Most CEOs recognize that no matter how much research and analysis is fed to them, there will always be room for more. "Finally you have to stop revving up the car and shove it in gear," says venture capitalist David Mahoney. He believes that the tendency to overanalyze business problems stems from a lack of confidence.

"It's a sign of insecurity," Mahoney says, "not of insufficient information." He compares the executive suffering from analysis paralysis to the housewife who keeps putting off giving a dinner party because she doesn't have just the right silverware and dishes. "But I'm a maverick," he confesses. "I get scared by all these planners and their belief that some guy with a set of numbers is going to bail us out."

Mahoney is hopeful that future research on the unconscious mind will reveal a few clues about what he considers are "intuition's deep secrets." Perhaps the David Mahoney Institute of Neurological Sciences at the University of Pennsylvania, which is endowed by him and devoted to studying the complexities of the brain, will contribute to that research. But in the meantime he urges business leaders to stop trying to analyze their hunches as they try to analyze everything else, and instead "follow them like the ancient navigators followed the stars. The voyage may be lonely," he says. "But the stars will take you where you want to go."

10

A TENTATIVE DIP IN THE COSMIC POOL

BECAUSE science has succeeded in explaining most observable phenomena, the far-out notion that intuition involves dipping into some kind of shared cosmic pool may be viewed skeptically. We all have a tendency to dismiss the unexplained as nonexistent. And so even when we personally experience an instance of mental telepathy, an example of clairvoyance, or simply a feeling of déjà vu, indicating the possibility of a connection between two people, objects, or events far apart, we tend to shrug them off as coincidence.

Yet psychologists, physicists, and molecular biologists are captivated by the shreds of evidence they see of some sort of energy link between everything in the universe. They are intrigued with the possibility that anything that happens is simultaneously encoded everywhere. This would make telepathy and clairvoyance more plausible because neither phenomenon would then depend on energy particles having to traverse time and space. Plausible or not, readers who find it troubling to take a quick figurative dip in this cosmic pool, or even a short speculative detour through a province still marked "paranormal" on maps of the human mind, should skip this chapter and proceed directly to Part IV.

Everything in this chapter is carried to speculative lengths. The theories elaborated on have only flimsy documentation to support them. Nevertheless, the notion of certain shared intuitive powers, still considered beyond human limits, should not be too disconcerting. After all, our estimates of human limits are constantly being revised. The

four-minute mile, once considered the ultimate speed limit
of the runner, is now routinely broken. Surely, what are still
regarded as the normal limits of the mind stand ready to be
broken too. And if a few of these far-out notions are
someday substantiated, they would help confirm the crucial
importance of an incubation period in the use of intuition.

The purpose of this chapter, then, is to at least glance at
some of the unproven reasons being offered by scientists
today for giving the mind a chance to contact sources not
reachable through the senses (extrasensory perception). Or
far more mind-boggling, to telepathically tap into that
limitless, timeless universal information bank, the so-called
cosmic pool. The connection between telepathy and intuition is obscure. But recognizing the existence of a cosmic
pool carries an interesting implication. It means that when
we obey the internal dictates of our own nature and rely on
intuition we are really acting under the influence of some
external web going back to the beginning of time.

If that is true, intuition is not influenced solely by past
personal experiences or repressed desires stored in our
subconscious. It is then also affected by extraneous vibes,
or whatever we call those murky telepathic communiqués
coming secondhand from other living creatures or emanating directly from an eternal pool. The celebrated Swiss
psychiatrist Carl Jung wrote of the "inherited powers of
imagination from time immemorial." He referred to primordial images that keep reappearing in myths and various
cultures as "archetypes," and used the word "synchronic-
ity" to describe coincidence of unrelated events. The claim
therefore could be made that at least part of our unconscious
consists of glimmerings either inherited from our ancestors
or acquired from our contemporaries. Not all of these
glimmerings serve us well. Joan of Arc was burned at the
stake for heeding the voices she heard.

MESSAGE FROM A MUMMY

Whether they are helpful or not, telepathic powers remain
pretty spooky and speculative. All that can be said with

assurance is that man seems to be susceptible to subtle sources of energy from both geophysical and human forces. And not just man. Animals also catch vibes. For instance, we know they run away anticipating the coming of an earthquake.

We know, too, that within every creature there is at least one biochemical link that could somehow serve as an information conduit. The double-helix molecule, DNA (deoxyribonucleic acid), delivers the heritage message to each species. Perhaps it carries other messages, too. In any case, it has tremendous survival powers, taking what it needs from the environment to multiply, and long outliving the body it inhabits. Recently some of this human genetic material was removed virtually undamaged from a twenty-four-hundred-year-old Egyptian mummy.

Because of DNA, considerable information is encoded in every creature's brain before birth. The young Canada goose doesn't have to be tutored in formation flying. And though we think of our own offspring as beginning a brand-new life, human babies aren't born with blank brains either. Even the unborn begin to learn before they leave the womb—to suck, drink, use their lungs and limbs, and to respond to sound, light, and touch. A growing number of obstetricians now fear that the effort made for many years to keep a pregnant woman's weight down may have undernourished the fetus, retarding prenatal brain development as well. "I believe every child is born a genius," Buckminster Fuller said facetiously. "They just get de-geniused very rapidly." He blamed overprotective parents for telling children: "Never mind what *you* think. Pay attention to *me!*" The effervescent Fuller also claimed that he made many mathematical discoveries during his lifetime. But he added: "I always had the most peculiar feeling that they were known before, somewhere, sometime in the universe." He called that sensation "intellectual mustiness."

Not such a musty idea. A provocative hypothesis has been advanced by British biologist Rupert Sheldrake that whenever a member of a species learns something new, the "causative field" or behavorial blueprint is altered. Then if the new behavior is repeated enough, a "morphic resonance" is established that will affect every member of the species. Perhaps Bucky Fuller plucked his seemingly new mathematical ideas from a morphic resonance lingering on from Archimedes, father of the Eureka factor.

Sheldrake himself is riding a resonant wave that has borne Asian mystics along for thousands of years. One of the fundamental tenets of Eastern philosophy is that each mind has access to the whole of a universal pattern. This intellectual interwovenness is the essence of the Chinese classic *I Ching*, the *Book of Changes*. Except in *I Ching*, the pattern has been elaborated into a system of ever-changing hexograms, composed of the primordial pair of opposites yin (negative) and yang (positive), from which the answers to all of life's questions presumably can be drawn.

Asian mystics describe the mind "turning on itself" and "viewing things beyond awareness," giving impetus to the importance of an incubation period of intuition. They insist that the works of man are incomplete unless they contain this higher insight, which may not be expressible in words. "He who knows does not speak. He who speaks does not know," said Lao-tzu, the ancient Chinese mystic and father of Taoism.

PARTNERS IN A COSMIC DANCE

In a fascinating book titled *The Tao of Physics*, Fritjof Capra paints a parallel picture of the unity expressed in Eastern philosophy and the interconnected web of sub-atomic physics. "Tao" means "reality" or the true "way of going." However, while most people envision a universe built on material reality, Capra depicts "dynamic patterns which do not exist as isolated entities, but as integral parts of an inseparable network of interactions." He thus describes the universe as engaged in a "continual cosmic dance of energy." Physicists boring in today on the possibility of a "unified field" are pursuing this notion still further. They are trying to prove that all of nature, including gravity, is reducible to one fundamental force.

Perhaps, then, telepathic information and subliminal impressions are themselves a single force. They both show up in the subconscious, possibly shaped by the same cosmic influences. Both, too, are received only when the mind is relaxed and in the mood. Hypnotists put the mind into a receptive state, and under their spell the unconscious can recall incredible detail. Most often, however, this receptive mood just occurs.

After *Jonathan Livingston Seagull* became a best-seller, author Richard Bach used to startle interviewers by announcing: "I didn't write this book." Asked who did, he would explain how he was walking alone along the waterfront in Long Beach, California, one evening when he heard a voice call out: "Jonathan Livingston Seagull." He felt that he had experienced something of special significance. But he was a beginning writer and didn't even have a typewriter. So scribbling rapidly in longhand on a yellow pad, he finished the first part of the story at one sitting.

Eleanor Friede, the book's editor, says Bach told her it was as if he were watching a movie. He saw this bird flying and wrote what he saw. Nothing had ever come to him that way before. Then suddenly the movie stopped and he had to stop writing. The movie didn't start up again for six years. But he woke up at 3 A.M. one day and the movie was running in his head again. He got up, went to the typewriter he owned by then, and finished the story. Bach still maintains that he didn't write the book but that it merely came "through" him.

Friede, who has become a believer in psychic phenomena, uses the word "matrix" to describe the confluence of forces she believes entered into the success of *Jonathan Livingston Seagull*. First, following a chance meeting with Bach, she salvaged the manuscript that two dozen publishers had already turned down. Then, as she explains, "the accompanying illustrations submitted by Bach were paintings of birds that looked as if they were stuffed." Macmillan wouldn't consider the expense of assigning a photographer. But by chance, photographer Russell Munson, an old friend of Bach's, had many years earlier won a special grant to photograph sea gulls. He had a box full of old negatives stashed away in his studio, where Bach slept when he came to New York. Munson agreed to let Bach use them for 20 percent of the royalties. Although the book's meager first edition sold out, Friede had to push Macmillan to go back on press. But what really convinces her now that this slender volume had some extra, inexplicable impetus behind it was the mystical power it seemed to exert over its readers.

REPORTS OF STRANGE JOURNEYS

Today Eleanor Friede publishes books as an independent producer. One of her favorite authors is Robert Monroe, whose first book, *Journeys Out of the Body*, became a cult classic in 1971 and whose second, *Far Journeys*, came out in 1985. Monroe has transited through several careers—and worlds, too, if you believe his published accounts. Originally an electronics engineer, he later produced, directed, wrote, and composed the background music for more than four hundred radio programs, including "Rocky Gordon," a popular railroad adventure series inspired by his own youthful stint as a hobo. Eventually he rose to vice president for programming at the Mutual Broadcasting System and later operated his own cable TV company in Virginia.

But Monroe began having strange, inexplicable experiences during his sleep. As he relates in *Journeys Out of the Body*, he found himself hovering ghostlike above his bed. In this detached, massless state, he claims, he was able with practice to pass through walls and travel down the street to visit sleeping friends and neighbors, gradually extending his nocturnal travels cross-country. In time, he reports, by inducing waves of vibration in his body even during waking hours, "I could unhook myself from the physical with ridiculous ease." Soon, Monroe writes, he was venturing much farther afield and visiting the dead in the realm of "infinity and eternity."

Finally giving up broadcasting for full-time study of OOBE (out-of-body experiences), he established the Monroe Institute of Applied Science in 1981 on 850 acres that he bought in the foothills of Virginia's Blue Ridge Mountains and named New Land. The key process employed there is Hemi-Sync, an acoustical system developed and patented by Monroe back in 1975 to induce OOBE.

Hemi-Sync creates this altered state of mind by introducing a slightly different sound-wave frequency into each ear, thus building a synchronized resonance between the two hemispheres of the brain. More than three thousand people have already visited the institute to undergo OOBE test hops in darkened cells called CHECs (Controlled Holistic Environmental Chambers) or to participate in brain-study workshops. Monroe now also markets Hemi-Sync sound-wave stereocassettes for relaxation, concentration, or for simply improving your golf or tennis game.

Eleanor Friede, who bought property and is building a country home at New Land, says that one problem Monroe faced in writing his new book, *Far Journeys*, was how to relay to readers what he claims was received by him in the world beyond via NVC (nonverbal communication). He describes NVC as "direct, instant experiencing, immediate knowing, transmitted from one intelligent energy system to another." Eventually, she explains, Monroe relayed the information in "thought balls," which precipitate intuition and understanding. Monroe's insights, says Friede, "will mean many things to many people, though those who require concrete proof will probably not go with them." But even Friede is hard-pressed to describe a thought ball. In *Far Journeys* a thought ball is defined as "a packet of thought/mentation, total memory."

Many distinguished scientists are discovering, as Monroe is convinced he did, that logic and common sense do not always help gain new insights into the functioning of the universe. Their thesis is that we are all components of a whole that may not be perceptible except through intuition. British physicist Brian Josephson won a Nobel Prize in 1973 for discovering particles that pass like ghosts through supposedly impenetrable barriers (just as Monroe claims his detached mind did during its nightly forays through his neighbors' homes). Today, instead of physics, Josephson is concentrating on psychic phenomena. He claims there are simply too many things "ordinary physics doesn't take into account."

THE SCIENTIFIC COMMUNITY'S OPENING MIND

The scientific community is now much more open-minded about psychic phenomena than it used to be. More than one hundred U.S. colleges currently offer courses in parapsychology, the quasi science that studies the interaction of mind and matter. A recent poll of medical school professors revealed that 58 percent of them favored the study of psychic phenomena, while 35 percent claimed they personally have had psychic experiences. According to a 1984 Gallup poll, about half of all Americans have had at least one experience they consider to be psychic.

There may not be a nationwide clamor to explain these experiences. Nevertheless, an increasing number of researchers are beginning to apply true scientific methods to pursuing one of man's most profound and ancient mysteries: the relationship of the mind to the physical world. Their studies include remote viewing (the ability to identify and sketch objects seen through the eyes of somebody miles away); precognition (the ability to know in advance); psychokinesis (the movement of physical objects using only the mind); OOBE; ESP; telepathy; and other forms of "psi," the psychological umbrella that covers all of those subtle information-processing systems that may someday enable us to transcend time, space, and the limited perception of our five senses.

One of the reasons parapsychology is gaining respect is new testing devices that eliminate the possibility of fraud or coincidence. The so-called random number generator uses the decay of radioactive atoms—an action beyond ordinary human control—to produce numerical readouts on a screen, which participants in various precognition experiments then try to guess. Robert Jahn, dean of Princeton University's school of engineering, has designed many of these testing machines. He has also conducted numerous experiments in remote viewing, which he says is of clear "interest for intelligence agencies, law enforcement units, and any other activity relying on surveillance." Recently he focused on the possibility of mental interaction with computers to determine if a person could psychically disrupt the memory function of a microchip, a remote possibility that has enormous implications for banks.

MILITARY ESP

Although the Department of Defense denies any interest in parapsychology, items keep showing up in the military budget under such headings as Novel Biological Information Transfer Systems, the military nomenclature for ESP. In his book *Mind Wars*, Ronald McRae reports that the Pentagon financed psychic research to study the so-called shell game basing mode for MX missiles, a system that would attempt to confuse Soviet military strategists by shifting the weapons among a number of concrete shelters.

Soviet scientists, in the race for military supremacy, have not slighted the study of intuition. They have probably been much more active than we have. At least they attach more significance to ESP than we do. Listen to Dr. Leonid Leonidovich Vasiliev, chairman of physiology at the University of Leningrad, winner of the Lenin Peace Prize, and the Soviets' main advocate of studying ESP for military purposes: "The discovery of energy underlying extrasensory perception," he declares, "will be the equivalent of the discovery of atomic energy."

Perhaps both the Pentagon and the Kremlin are heeding the advice of Sigmund Freud, who wrote near the end of his illustrious career: "If I had my life to live over again, I should devote myself to psychical research rather than psychoanalysis." Freud was not alone in that feeling. His contemporary Carl Jung wrote: "Even physics, the strictest of all applied sciences, depends to an astonishing degree upon intuition, which works by way of the unconscious."

FISSION IN THE MARKETPLACE

Businessmen, naturally, are less interested in the scientist's efforts to unravel the mysteries of intuition than they are in applying the results. The views of Dr. Solomon Dutka, however, are particularly pertinent because he has had a foot in both camps. As a nuclear physicist, he worked for the Manhattan Project during World War II, helping to develop the atomic bomb. Today he heads a large international marketing research firm, Audits & Surveys Inc., which assists companies like Coca-Cola and Ford in testing public reaction to new products and concepts. "Your own universe," says Dutka, "determines the kind of intuition you need. The scientist struggles to unlock nature's secrets. But nature is passive and uncapricious. It doesn't take advantage of a missed opportunity. The businessman struggling to make a buck in a chaotically competitive arena faces capriciously changing demographics. He's suddenly out of business if he doesn't sense the right thing to do."

Dutka also claims that scientists are instinctively conservative, viewing what they see in terms of the past. "They saw the automobile as a horseless carriage," he says. "Even after they took the horse away and inserted the gasoline engine, they rated that forevermore in horsepower, just as they still measure the brightness of the incandescent bulb in candlepower." Business leaders, Dutka believes, are more positive and forwardlooking, intuitively realizing there is no status quo. "To succeed," he says, "they have to make things happen. Even if it means convincing customers that some new fancy-named placebo will make them feel better."

In his book *Revolution in Science*, I. Bernard Cohen writes: "Every scientist has a vested interest in the preservation of the status quo to the extent that he does not want the skills and expert knowledge which he has acquired at great cost in time and learning energy to become obsolete." Cohen makes it understandable why physicists and molecular biologists, like political right-wingers, would therefore seek to suppress revolutionary movements within their sciences. But even so, the possibility of human minds resonating in various ways with each other and with the impulses of nature is currently being pursued by many members of the scientific community. The scientists seem to be following in the wake of the mystics and poets.

INFINITY IN THE PALM OF YOUR HAND

Down through the ages the poet has been telling us all, whether we are devoted to science, business, or the arts, that "no man is an island," that nothing happens in isolation, that we live and die on cosmic cues. The mystic, too, has told us that all things and events are creations of the mind, arising from a particular state of consciousness, and dissolving again if the state is transcended. "Let go of limited consciousness in favor of a vastly expanded one," the Buddhists recommend. This same view is beautifully expressed in William Blake's famous lines:

> To see a world in a grain of sand,
> And a heaven in a wild flower,
> Hold infinity in the palm of your hand,
> And eternity in an hour.

The idea of the intuitive mind tapping into a cosmic pool and drawing on sources not available to the senses will intrigue us for an eternity to come. There is indeed a world to explore in every grain of sand or drop of DNA. But the greatest discoveries are made when the mind turns inward and views things beyond awareness—the best argument for providing an incubation period that can spark intuition. The hard part of this interior viewing process always is discerning the difference between those instantaneous, illuminating flashes that perceive a new truth and the shadows of illusion that can be just as intriguing and appear just as real.

IV

ILLUMINATION

11

EUREKA, I'VE GOT IT!

INTUITIVE flashes come day or night, even in the middle of a sound sleep. They come in a conference, on a hike, at the opera, during a party, down in a subway, or up in a plane, but most often while you're concentrating on something else. Inventor Art Fry of 3M was singing in a choir and needed bookmarks that wouldn't fall out of his hymnal when he got the idea for Post-it notes, those ubiquitous, peelable little yellow memos with a strip of stickum on the back. The crucial point is *don't tune out your hunch*. Don't let Monitor, the logical left hemisphere of your brain, talk you out of a sudden intuitive perception.

It's easy to intellectualize or analyze your way out of heeding a hunch. The trouble is you *know*, but you don't know how you know. So remind yourself that this fleeting feeling, this little whisper from deep inside your brain, may contain far more information—both facts and impressions—than you're likely to obtain from hours of analysis.

As was discussed in the last chapter, very possibly some vast substratum of experience has been scratched. Only lightly, perhaps. Often not sharply enough for you to describe the sensation. But don't fret if you can't convert those vibes into something verbal. The Zen Buddhist knows that words imprison thoughts, though he won't tell you so because he doesn't believe in giving explanations.

Finally, before ignoring that faint internal whisper, tell yourself one last time that your surest, best, most potentially profitable hunch will be wasted if you don't have the guts to follow a gut feeling.

Eurekas are also referred to as the "Aha response" and are often followed by a "Now I see the picture!" exclamation. But the picture quickly fades, since those faint and fleeting internal signals emanating from Mover are easily suppressed. Logic can always smother a hunch if it's allowed to. Opposing arguments readily spring to mind, and they sound something like this: "Be sensible. Important breakthroughs don't just happen. Progress is incremental. It evolves from slow, step-by-step study, often requiring carefully integrated teamwork carried on for weeks or years."

Of course, that's old Monitor talking. Don't listen. Or at least don't be too easily swayed. Remember, Monitor feeds on the fears and self-doubts accumulated over a lifetime. In spite of everything Monitor says, humankind has been catapulted ahead ten, twenty, or a hundred years at a crack by visions that were experienced instantaneously. Civilization's great clarifications did not follow from either small tiptoeing steps or massive brainstorming assaults, but from deep inexplicable insights. Einstein, who found that his thoughts often crystallized best while he was drifting about in a canoe, attributed his theory of relativity to a sudden realization of how time and space are inextricably intertwined. "The really valuable factor was intuition," he said.

But intuitive insights are valueless if they are automatically dismissed. One way of combatting Monitor and staying receptive to those sudden flashes is to encourage certain activities and conditions during which they seem to occur. There are no firm rules for profiting from the Eureka factor. However, realizing under what circumstances valuable discoveries have blossomed in the minds of others should help you to understand that those business hunches are more than blind faith.

PROCESS VERSUS EVENT

Dr. Jonas Salk contends that you can't isolate one piece of the creative process as the precise moment of discovery.

"People have some idea that discovery is fallen upon," he says, "that it's something you find. That's not how it happens. Discovery is a quest. You perceive it by questing. But it's not unnatural for a discovery to be made and the significance of it to be realized much later."

If people ask him to pinpoint when he finally hit upon the antipolio vaccine that bears his name, he responds testily that they don't comprehend creativity. "There is a moment of conception, and a moment of birth," he says. "But between them is a long period of gestation," which is all part of the discovery process.

"In 1936," Salk explains, "somebody said something that seemed paradoxical to me—meaning that the two things that were said didn't fit together. They had to do with whether or not you had to experience infection in order to develop immunity to a virus disease. I put that in the back of my mind.

"Then in 1939, I found myself in a laboratory that was working on influenza. So that idea came back to me, and there was an opportunity to test it. I asked nature the question, 'Is it or is it not true that you must first be infected to become immune?' And nature said, 'Go ahead and design the right experiment.' I designed a series of experiments and the answer came back, 'Yes, it is possible to become immune without being infected.' You see, the answer preexists. What people think of as the moment of discovery is really the discovery of the question."

LISTENING TO YOURSELF

As Dr. Salk attests, the dialogue between Monitor and Mover can be highly constructive. It doesn't have to end negatively with Monitor automatically dismissing every fresh insight. As he says: "Talking out a series of scenarios can produce a new perspective." Early in his career, Salk reports, he imagined himself as an immune system and then asked what he would do to combat a virus or cancer cell. On the basis of those early conversations with himself, he began constructing hundreds of tedious laboratory experiments to come up with the answers—including those that eventually yielded his vaccine. "But long before that," says Salk, "this internal dialogue became second nature to me. I found my mind worked this way all the time. Others may not be conscious that they conduct this kind of dialogue, but they do. Why should it only happen to me?"

Conrad Hilton, whose intuitive moves in the hotel business were legend, writes in his book, *Be My Guest,* "I know when I have a problem and have done all I can to figure it, I keep listening in a sort of inside silence 'til something clicks and I feel a right answer."

Developer Jim Rouse reports that before he undertook building from scratch the city of Columbia, Maryland, he kept asking himself questions: "Do cities really have to grow badly? Does urban sprawl and clutter really have to be?" And like Salk, he concluded: "When you ask the question, it evokes an answer." So in 1962 he constructed a model in his mind of what Columbia would be like. During the next year he obtained financing from Connecticut General Insurance Company and bought 165 farms, assembling the land. "Today," glows Rouse, "we're a city of seventy thousand people, with thirty-eight thousand jobs and eighteen hundred businesses. We did far better than anybody could have possibly forecast. The county officials were a nervous wreck. Even I sometimes heard a voice saying it couldn't be done."

In *The Inner Game of Tennis,* author Gallwey describes the dialogue that goes on in the head of most players as a running conversation between the "conscious teller, Self 1" (Monitor), and the "unconscious, automatic doer, Self 2" (Mover). Self 1 can throw any player off his spontaneous best game, advises Gallwey, by shouting a stream of instructions: "Okay, dammit, keep your stupid wrist firm."

Salk says his internal dialogues have now shifted from immunity to creativity. "Both," he says, "are important natural phenomena." In the more recent conversations with himself he has come to recognize the origin of his two internal voices. "Intuition is the voice of my *self*" (or Mover), he says. "Reason is the voice of *me* or *I*" (or

Monitor). "So I am two, not one. I serve my *self*, but very frequently *I* have to get out of the way of my *self*."

TRUSTING YOUR HUNCH

During internal conversations it is necessary to keep reminding yourself that the Eureka factor requires trust to work. Says Salk: "It is always with excitement that I wake up in the morning wondering what my intuition will toss up to me, like gifts from the sea. I work with it and rely upon it. It's my partner."

It doesn't bother Salk that intuition, as he says, "is something we don't quite understand the biology of yet." He calls intuition the "poetic part of intellect," and he quotes from Elizabeth Sewell's *Orpheus* to prove his point: "The mind knows in poems a little more than it knows it knows. A poem will often tell the thinking mind where to think next."

RIDDING YOURSELF OF PRECONCEPTIONS

Often it is some inexplicable impulse, some quirk of fate, that nudges the mind in a new direction. The key moment in the search for the structure of the DNA molecule came when codiscoverer James Watson was manipulating the components of a model molecule, trying to fit them together in different ways. He and his research partner, Francis Crick, had always assumed, as had other scientists, that each segment had to be paired with its twin. "Suddenly," reported Watson, "I became aware . . . that both pairs could be flip-flopped and still have their . . . bonds facing in the same direction. It strongly suggested that the backbones of the two chains run in opposite directions." That instantaneous realization triggered the discovery of the famous double helix.

We all pay tribute to names like Crick and Watson. But then, as Polaroid's founder Edwin Land wrote years ago, "we fail to learn the lesson that their names teach." That lesson, Land explained, is our need to "slough off the tentacles of the group mind." The New England entrepreneur, out of whose own intuition came nonglare Polaroid glass, instant film, and the instant camera, maintained that every significant step in every field "is taken by some individual who has freed himself from a way of thinking that is held by friends and associates who may be more intelligent, better educated, better disciplined, but who have not mastered the art of the fresh, clean look at old, old knowledge."

STOP QUESTIONING YOUR QUALIFICATIONS

An analysis of fifty-eight major twentieth-century inventions, from chemicals to computers to ballpoint pens, reveals that in forty-six of those discoveries the inventor was an individual, a small firm, or somebody in the "wrong business." King Gillette, the inventor of the safety razor, was a cork salesman. George Eastman, when he revolutionized photography, was a bookkeeper, while a couple of musicians invented Kodachrome. John Dunlop, coinventor of the pneumatic tire, was a veterinarian. The automatic telephone dialing system was invented by an undertaker, and a watchmaker trying to solve a brass fitting problem came up with continuous casting steel. The soapmakers ignored detergents and the dyemakers invented them instead, while the aircraft engine manufacturers repeatedly spurned the jet, leaving its development to the airframe makers.

What does this teach us about the Eureka factor? It shows that inexperience may make us more daring, and that a fearless, facile challenger can dethrone the stolid, established champ—sometimes with the simplest idea. It illustrates, too, how an entrenched bunker mentality makes a defender vulnerable to an aggressive, innovative attacker.

Solomon Dutka, the atomic scientist turned market analyzer whose company, Audits & Surveys, was mentioned in the previous chapter, relates how a former client of his in the fountain pen business refused to recognize reports of the inroads being made by ballpoint manufacturers. "The client said, 'I make fountain pens, not ballpoints,' reiterating his high percentage of total fountain pen sales. He couldn't see the significance of an overall writing instrument market that was moving away from him."

But, according to Dutka, that bunker mentality, while still typical of the scientist, is no longer commonplace in marketing. "The scientist," he says, "survives by defending his point of view. But the CEO knows he'll soon be out of business if he looks at the world that way."

RISKING AN EDUCATED GUESS

Executives tend to view scientists as objective thinkers, puttering around hermetically sealed laboratories in pursuit of facts. Many scientists conform to this image. But in science, as in business, the rules of objectivity apply only to the way ideas are tested. Discovery works differently. From Copernicus to Einstein, scientists making important break-throughs have refuted, not supported, what were assumed to be facts. And very unscientifically. "Time and again," cites University of Wisconsin physicist Robert Marsh, "a re-markable pattern of discovery has repeated itself: a lucky guess based on shaky arguments and absurd ad hoc assump-tions gives a formula that turns out to be right, though at first no one can see why on earth it should be."

The same kind of "shaky arguments" and "absurd assumptions" sometimes blossom into business inspira-tions. Who would have thought that a seat-of-the-pants combat pilot would return from Vietnam with the overnight Federal Express mail system tucked away in his head and beat the U.S. Postal Service at its own business?

LETTING YOUR MIND PLAY

In 1983 Jonas Salk wrote a slender book published by the Columbia University Press called the *Anatomy of Reality: Merging of Intuition and Reason*. In it he provides further evidence of the delicate balance between inspiration and logic that is required for the Eureka factor to function. "A new way of thinking is now needed to deal with our present reality," he writes. "Our subjective responses (intuitional) are more sensitive and more rapid than our objective responses (reasoned). This is the nature of the way the mind works. We first sense and then we reason why." But, adds Salk, "intuition must be allowed a free rein and be allowed to play."

When J.P. Morgan couldn't make a decision, he would put the problem out of his mind by getting out a pack of cards and playing solitaire for an hour.

Eurekas have, indeed, occurred while the mind is at play. John J. Moran, a onetime lab technician, made a fortune by inventing an automatic blood analyzer in 1965. For months he had worked unsuccessfully trying to design the machine. Finally, in frustration he embarked on a long-postponed vacation. On his first day away, as the sun's rays filtered through the hotel room window onto his face, he saw in his mind's eye a detailed picture of the machine. He sprang from bed, hastily sketched a diagram on hotel stationery, and flew home, spending the next few months building a prototype from the sketch. The prototype worked perfectly, and Moran built around it a company called Hycel Inc., which he sold to a German conglomerate in 1979 for $40 million.

LOOKING FOR ANALOGIES

Intuitive flashes like Moran's can be the catalyst for the growth of any organization. Sometimes the Eureka factor results in a totally new technology or product, other times in a new marketing strategy. In either case, the result can be a clear, competitive edge. It is not surprising, therefore, that industrial psychologists, armed with new knowledge of the brain, have been striving to unravel the mysteries of the Eureka factor. More than half of the Fortune 500 companies, including Procter & Gamble, IBM, Shell, and Singer, have undertaken some kind of creativity experiments or training.

In the course of these studies, some of history's most notable new findings have been reviewed to determine if a pattern of discovery could be discerned. In many cases the intuitive spark was traced to an analogy. Einstein struck upon his theory of relativity while riding on a train and absently watching another train pull ahead at a faster speed, giving him the sense of moving backward—relatively. Louis Pasteur concluded that bodily infection was caused by external microorganisms after observing that grapes would ferment only if their skin was broken. Until then it was assumed that infection stemmed from internal gases. Analogies stir new ideas and concepts using concrete images rather than abstractions. They create other concrete images so that an idea flow proceeds spontaneously. In fact, the analogy can be played around with again and again in the light of the original image.

Fascinating new insights about the power of analogy are emerging from a twenty-year, $6 million study at Rutgers University of the 3.5 million pages of notebooks and letters left by Thomas Edison. "These documents give us entry into the mind of one of the world's most creative people," says Dr. Reese Jenkins, director of the study. "They also tell a lot about the essence of invention itself." Edison is created with 1,093 patents; no other individual has ever invented more. So no one, it was assumed, had experienced more flashes of brilliance, accompanied, perhaps, by more cries of "Eureka!"

The revised portrait of Edison reveals a mind frequently reaching for an analogy. For example, the early drawings of his kinetoscope, a prototype motion picture projector, prove that it evolved from his already successful phonograph. "I am experimenting upon an instrument which does for the eye what the phonograph does for the ear," he wrote. Similarly, sketches of early versions of the incandescent bulb reveal an electric-current regulator taken from the telegraph.

NOT FEARING FAILURE

We all know that fear is corrosive. It blocks insights and keeps self-confidence from being converted into action. As

Fran Tarkenton says: "Winning means being unafraid to lose." But winning or losing a game depends also on many external factors, including the confidence of your opponent. However, confidence in yourself and in your intuitive insights is not constantly on the line and dependent on every performance as it is in sports. Coming to realize this is liberating because it allows you to take chances, to follow your hunches and commit to new ideas.

Debbi Fields says that when she was twenty years old and starting out in the cookie business, all of the professional marketing people she consulted said it was a bad idea. Even her friends told her she was going to fail. "So I went in totally petrified," she says. "But then I said to myself, if it's not meant to be that's perfectly all right. I knew I wouldn't be able to live with myself thinking if I had only stopped listening to everybody else and just gone out and done it."

HEEDING YOUR DREAMS

Dreams, sometimes described by psychoanalysts as "seepage from the subconscious," have for a long time been recognized for their role in precipitating discovery. Otto Loewi, who shared the 1936 Nobel Prize in physiology or medicine, dreamed of a way to prove his theory about the chemical transmission of nerve impulses. But when he woke up, he couldn't recall the dream clearly enough to perform the experiment. Fortunately, the dream recurred the next night and he was able to rush to the lab to verify his concept. Eventually, Loewi found that he had jotted down a description of the experiment years before but had forgotten it.

Years ago, when Conrad Hilton decided to buy the Stevens House, now the Chicago Hilton, he submitted a sealed bid of $165,000. But the following morning he awakened with the amount $180,000 stuck in his head, so he changed his bid. The second highest bid, it turned out, was $179,800.

In 1985, when treasure hunter Mel Fisher finally found the Spanish galleon *Nuestra Señora de Atocha*, which sank three centuries ago in a hurricane off the Florida Keys laden with gold and silver, he was following a dream once had by his son Dirk. Dirk had drowned in 1975 while searching for the *Atocha* on a shallow underwater reef where three silver bars from the galleon had already been located. But that earlier find proved to be misleading. Ten years were spent following a teasing trail of artifacts and ballast back toward the reef, crisscrossing thousands of acres of ocean floor. "It was Dirk who was convinced that the *Atocha* was in deeper waters," revealed one of Fisher's divers. "He had a dream about the *Atocha*, a very vivid dream that told him the treasure was where they first looked. There was nothing logical about it, but Dirk's death and the dream convinced Mel to search again in deeper waters."

The classic case of literally dreaming up a solution, and a story often cited by science history buffs, is that of Elias Howe's invention of the sewing machine. One night, exhausted by false starts trying to solve the problem of connecting needle, thread, and material, he fell asleep and dreamed of being captured by cannibals. He envisioned himself trussed up in a kettle with the fire laid, being warned to solve his sewing-machine problem or be cooked alive. As the cannibals danced chanting around the kettle, Howe spotted holes in the tips of their spears. Jolted awake, he realized that if he threaded the needle at the point, his sewing machine would work. Psychiatrists urge us all to pay close attention to the details of our dreams. They may contain solutions to our problems.

Daydreaming, too, abets the discovery process. In his book *Intrapreneuring*, author Gifford Pinchot III describes how Hulki Aldikacti, the former chief engineer responsible for Pontiac's highly successful Fiero sports car, first built a wooden mock-up of the cockpit. To feel what the finished car would be like, he used to sit fantasizing in the driver's seat during coffee breaks. Writes Pinchot:

This behavior is absolutely typical of intrapreneurs. Since one of their most basic tools is daydreaming, their natural inclination in any spare moment is to play over a new

business opportunity in their mind's eye, considering the
many different ways to go forward and the barriers they
might encounter along each path. Because they foresee
barriers, intrapreneurs can plan ways around them before
becoming locked into a death struggle with an unwork-
able situation.

TURNING AROUND ADVERSITY

There are many such instances of business leaders relying
on intuition for a protective nudge to circumvent obstacles
or to avert disaster. Intuition inspired Ross Perot, the
iconoclastic chairman of Electronic Data Systems, to orga-
nize the secret rescue mission that liberated the imprisoned
EDS employees in Iran. "Everybody thought it was 'mission impossible,'" says Perot. "But I knew my mind
wouldn't rest until those men were free." The feisty
Annapolis grad claims: "Throughout my career, the things
I've done best are the things people told me couldn't be
done."

A number of outside kibitzers, for instance, insisted that
Perot's decision to let General Motors acquire EDS spelled
big trouble. Merging with the automobile monolith meant
joining two distinctly different corporate cultures. There
was an arrogance abut Perot and his executives, all right,
that rankled the seven thousand GM data processing troops
transferred to EDS. As Perot himself admits: "There are no
job descriptions in this company. Anyone who wants one, I
give it to him personally. It's three words: 'Use your
head.'" This high-handed attitude could have kept the two
organizations from successfully meshing.

Still, Perot intuitively sensed that he and GM's boss,
Roger Smith, were both venturesome and creative enough
to bridge that corporate divide and to integrate their two
corporations. "If you want to get an elephant to move, then
you have to know where the sensitive spots are," says the
outspoken Perot about the big and cumbersome GM organization. "Roger knows where they are. In fact, he knows
how to get that elephant to dance."

John Teets, Greyhound Corporation's innovative chairman, whose mild manner masks a tough character, let intuition guide him into paring down that cumbersome conglomerate to make it more profitable. Greyhound's perennial problem child was Armour, a $2.5 billion subcorporation burdened with debt. "We contacted all the investment bankers," says Teets, "but they said, 'You'll never sell it. There are no buyers out there. All the meat companies are going into Chapter Eleven.'"

Teets, however, listened instead to a visceral voice that whispered: "Uncomplicate things. If you're ever going to sell Armour, first you have to make it understandable to all the analysts." The solution he struck on was to pump all the debt up to the parent company, though he recalls that "our own financial people fought me all the way to the board." Once the debt was cleaned up, he divided Armour into two profit centers: Armour-Dial, the soap company, which Greyhound kept; and Armour Foods, which it sold to ConAgra Inc. for $166 million. "Now that the deal's done," says Teets, "everybody says, 'Why, that's common sense. Why wasn't it done before?'"

Continental Airlines chairman Francisco Anthony Lorenzo, once a wide-bodied executive with a reputation for remoteness, slimmed forty-five pounds from his bulging corpus and became just plain Frank. Now a sleek, smooth-running marathoner, he is working the same metamorphosis on his once-bankrupt company. Resurrected as the New Continental, but with its salaries, fares, and route system slashed, the Houston-based carrier is turning a tidy profit. It became the first big airline to defy both a multiunion strike and the gravity of bankruptcy, so to speak, by staying in the sky.

The intuitive juggling act that it took to keep Continental's fleet in the air is a speciality of Lorenzo's. The son of a hairdresser who immigrated from Spain, he got to the top not by ascending a managerial hierarchy but by being an imaginative entrepreneur. His special flair is parlaying a small airline stake into enough stock to run the whole show. As a result, he is now chairman or president or both of three publicly owned aviation companies besides Continental: Texas Air Corporation, New York Air, and Jet Capital Corporation.

Lorenzo also came close to taking over two more airlines. He made a bid for National Airlines in 1978. Pan American won out, but Lorenzo's company pocketed a $47 million profit from the sale of its National stock. Then in 1985, he appeared to have picked off TWA. This time he lost out to Carl Icahn, but Lorenzo's Texas Air made away with another $50 million profit from that near miss. The launching pad for all this entrepreneurial action was an obscure firm he founded in 1966 with a Harvard Business School classmate, Robert Carney. Each invested $1,000.

Lorenzo equates intuition with vision. "I see chief executives in this business who just operate and never look ahead," he says. "A CEO's job is divided into two areas: to look into the future and interpret trends, and to steer the company as strongly as possible on the basis of what's coming."

A FEW CONCLUSIONS ABOUT THE EUREKA FACTOR

It is difficult to generalize about how intuition leads to new business conquests or helps turn adversity around. But examining some of the traits exhibited by the CEOs included in this chapter casts a little more light on how the Eureka factor functions.

First, as Lorenzo so clearly demonstrates, these leaders are more perceptive than reactive. Overall views of their businesses fascinate them much more than the specific problems their companies face. Although they absorb the big picture first, eventually they focus on smaller and smaller parts. Unintuitive managers seem to operate in reverse, first spotting the details that need fixing and then recommending incremental improvements.

Some intuitive decisions, like John Teets's idea of pumping the debt out of Armour into the parent Greyhound Corporation to make the subsidiary meat company more salable, do not appear rational at first, which is why the financiers fought him. But then, synergy by definition is nonrational because it carries you beyond the sum of the parts. However, the synergistic benefits don't usually become apparent until after the action is completed.

Leaders-to-be, while subconsciously synthesizing the bits of data and experience that can eventually propel them to the top, may not recognize the path to power, even though they are already on it. Debbi Fields didn't realize she was launching a big business. She now recalls a few amorphous feelings spurring her on, like "the urge to satisfy my emotional needs," and "my determination to give every customer personal service" (that's why Mrs. Fields employees, even the accountants, are required to start work in a cookie store), which hardly explain her phenomenal success. But her naive willingness to attempt the impossible (plus the help of a financially savvy husband) transported her magically from junior college dropout to founding mother of America's biggest cookie store chain.

The more leaders construct a neatly logical and coherent strategy, the less likely they are to explore all possibilities, including "thinking the unthinkable." John Teets ignored the conventional wisdom of his advisers and instead embarked on radical reorganizations that changed the whole thrust of Greyhound. But then, exponents of creative thinking have long advocated getting away from step-by-step vertical thinking and taking imaginative lateral leaps.

Intuitive executives accept as inevitable the essential mystery and ambivalence of the business world. Those inherent unknowns and contradictions never cease to produce surprises that keep catching traditional leaders off guard. But, in TV parlance, a "voice-over" seems to provide intuitive managers with the necessary answers that elude their peers. These inspired leaders also demonstrate an uncommon capacity for integrating a wealth of chaotic experiences into a keen, sure sense of homing in on a positive new course of action.

Whereas many leaders tend to underreact to mild stimuli and overreact to strong ones, the intuitive CEO senses the proper response. Ross Perot's response to the imprisonment of EDS employees in Iran inspired not only a daring rescue mission but also the best-seller *On Wings of Eagles*. It could be said that he and other intuitive CEO's today are the eagles of business. They take soaring flights of imagination instead of methodically piling fact upon fact in building an enterprise and its policies.

12

THE CRUCIAL
ELEMENT: TIMING

TIMING is an intrinsic part of intuition, the key element in capitalizing on the Eureka factor. "Intuition is sensing the right moment to make your move," says Robert P. Jensen, who once was a tight end for the Baltimore Colts and is now chairman of E.F. Hutton LBO Inc., the leveraged buyout arm of the brokerage firm that is located in Santa Barbara, California. "Some executives have a sixth sense that tells them, 'Now is the right time to do it.' You don't get that out of analysis or number-crunching at a computer."

Ill-timed—either premature or tardy—even the most creative ideas fall flat. Protective instincts also depend on knowing precisely when to act. Given insufficient lead time to take effect, a farseeing preventive move can end in disaster, a victim of *Titanic* syndrome. The doomed ship's captain, after all, had taken the prescribed precaution of posting a lookout in the bow. He simply failed to reckon on the time it would take the lumbering ocean liner to slow down to avoid hitting an iceberg.

Captaining a company and steering clear of economic icebergs involves more nebulous talents than running a taut ship. Even the most careful chief executive may be forced to respond rapidly on instinct to keep the enterprise afloat. Jensen is an engineer not ordinarily given to precipitate decisions. And he calls patience "a part of the intuitive process." Yet he recognizes the need for speed in "crisis management"—in responding to fierce competitors, or in passing so-called shark repellent measures to avert a hostile takeover. Carl Menk, chairman of the New York executive search firm Canny, Bowen Inc., observes that many old-style CEOs—highly successful operators in more stable times—are opting to step aside. "They lack the responsiveness and timing needed to cope with the greenmail threat, the consumer pressures, and the new goldfish-bowl exposure that puts their job under public scrutiny," claims Menk. "A CEO now has to sense intuitively what the public is thinking every minute of the day."

Speed, or simply lead time, in launching new products also requires gambling on a hunch. The intuitive boss knows that he can't always wait for the numbers or for the input of associates. As we learned in the last chapter, those "eagles" who soar off sooner and higher on inspired flights of fancy than the other birds in business seem guided by some kind of magical internal radar that not only determines their destination but their timing as well.

Kenneth Oshman, cofounder of Rolm Corporation, acquired by IBM in 1984, believes a chief executive's job is to peer intently three to five years into the future, looking for problems. In 1971 the first flicker of future trouble for Rolm spurred him into action. Rolm was then still a fast-growing maker of heavy-duty computers. But orders from the Defense Department, Rolm's biggest customer, looked as if they might slacken. Oshman decided to explore the new market for computerized telephone equipment, even though at first that opportunity didn't appear very fruitful. "But we didn't have a strong enough gut feeling that anything else was right for us," he told *Fortune*. "So we decided to see how we could turn this into a business."

By developing computer-controlled switching equipment that was far more sophisticated than anything AT&T or its competitors had, Rolm created a thriving new business. The company grew from annual sales of $1.5 million in 1971, when Oshman first sensed trouble ahead, to $660 million just before IBM acquired it. But the premise that set the whole logical process in motion turned out to be wrong. Rolm's military market for computers also continued to expand. Said Oshman: "I'd rather be lucky than right."

Jensen believes that professional athletes frequently demonstrate what appears to be lucky timing while they're performing. (Remember Bobby Thomson's ninth-inning, three-run homer in the final game of a three-game play-off that won the pennant for the old New York Giants in 1951?) "Now, does the businessman show this same intuitive sense when he's performing? I think so," says Jensen, who also believes that while his sense of the right moment to make a move in both business and football was improved by practice, "part of it comes with the genes. If you don't start with some of these instincts, there's no way you can develop them," he adds.

THE FRAGILE GIFT OF GOOD TIMING

The metamorphosis of Sherry Lansing from math teacher to movie magnate is an example of this gift of good timing. "I've always known when to leave a job and when to say," she says, though part of her climb to success seemed to occur magically, as if what Indian mystics call *Siddhis* were also at work. *Siddhis,* incidentally, are strange powers that enable people to perform impossible feats, sort of a Eureka factor carried to extremes. In any case, Lansing's inherent facility for being in the right spot at the right time beats most Hollywood scripts.

A beautiful young Northwestern University graduate goes to Los Angeles to teach high school math in Watts, a black neighborhood still seething from the 1965 riots. Three years later she becomes a model—a Max Factor girl—and then an actress. After a three-word (Hurry up, Nicky") walk-on part in *Funny Girl,* she plays opposite John Wayne in *Rio Lobo.* Her big moment comes when she walks off into the sunset with the Duke. But before that happens, during her six weeks on the set she comes to realize there are producers, directors, and all kinds of business wheeler-dealers in the movies besides actors. So she gives up acting, takes courses at UCLA in moviemaking, and lands a job as a script reader. After six years she gets to be senior vice president of production at Columbia Pictures, taking personal control of two big money-makers: *The China Syndrome* and *Kramer vs. Kramer*. Still, she has doubts, she admits, "that in my lifetime I'll ever see a woman as president of a movie company." Within a year Twentieth Century-Fox does pick a thirty-five-year-old woman president. It's Sherry Lansing, of course. Fade-out. End of movie.

Although Lansing no longer holds that exalted position, she attributes her meteoric rise to timing, intuition, and luck. "I'm a believer in destiny," she says. "All my life I had a passion for movies. But I had no idea how to get into the business." At first she only wanted to be an actress. Surprisingly, she found she didn't like it. "I wasn't comfortable playing anybody else," she admits. "I couldn't pretend." She believes that this inability to disguise her gut feelings is what has made her so decisive about changing jobs. "These same gut feelings," she says, "tell me which screenplay will make the best films."

Three years after she took command of Twentieth Century, Marvin Davis, the Denver oil wildcatter, bought the company. He tried to persuade her to stay. She mumbled excuses about not wanting to get up at 6 A.M. and work till midnight anymore, and about being "ready for a new challenge." But an internal voice was telling her to move on. Again, Lansing followed her intuition and left her $300,000-a-year post. "Good timing means knowing when to step down as well as up," she says, Eventually, she formed an independent production company at Paramount with Stanley Jaffe.

SENSING WHEN TO POUNCE AND WHEN TO PULL BACK

The gift of good timing depends on more than hearing opportunity knocking. It means being able to catch the sound of the first faint tap. Ted Turner may be better known for his mouth than his ears, but he has pounced successfully on a whole series of opportunities that others missed. In becoming owner of the Turner Broadcasting System, the

Atlanta Braves, and the Atlanta Hawks, and winner of the America's Cup in 1977—when he was dubbed Captain Outrageous—Turner demonstrated a sense of timing considered just about flawless. At age twenty-four he reversed the fortunes of his father's virtually bankrupt billboard company. In 1970 he bought a two-bit UHF station, WTBS, and built it into the country's largest cable "superstation." And in 1980 he started from scratch a twenty-four-hour cable news service, CNN, which confounded every prediction and crushed the competition. Eventually the time arrived, Turner felt, to make his big move. "I'd like to get my hands on a network," he announced publicly in 1983. "I'd like to be the big guy for a while."

Two years later, however, he stubbed his toe trying to carry off the whole Columbia Broadcasting System kicking and screaming. At first Turner's timing seemed sharp as ever, even if the junk bonds he offered CBS shareholders in exchange for their stock looked a little frayed around the edges. The network appeared vulnerable, having just been openly bruised by the libel suit brought by General William Westmoreland. More important, the price of its stock was undervalued. But a born sense of timing doesn't work without the financing to back it up, and in the end Turner had to abort his bid. He didn't even go down swinging. The man who had blasted TV network fare as "garbage" tried to put a better face on his misguided takeover attempt. "What am I but a free-enterprise guy," he said lamely. "The same as Bill Paley when he started CBS."

So why did the bombastic Turner time his big move before he had the wherewithal to carry it off? His mother, Florence Turner, may have hit on the answer. "He always needed a challenge," she told *Inc.* magazine. "At an early age it was obvious he was gifted. He had a lot of energy, and if it wasn't channeled productively he would get into mischief."

Says CBS chairman Tom Wyman, who won't be drawn into a discussion about Ted Turner's ill-timed attack: "Often, I suppose, great intuitive decisions are not to do things." Sensing when a move probably won't succeed is, after all, the flip side of good timing.

TIMING IN A MERCURIAL MARKETPLACE

If necessity is invention's mother, in today's fickle world, economic volatility is its father. That puts even more of a premium on intuitive timing. The Dreyfus Corporation's chairman, Howard Stein, believes that conditions change so abruptly in today's financial markets that gathering his key executives together and talking about timing has become much more important than planning. "As soon as you try to figure out what the various economic signals mean," he cautions, "something else starts happening. All I know is, things don't work like they used to work. So don't plan on doing anything based on the past."

Sensing that Dreyfus has to be more than just a picker of stocks in the present inhospitable financial environment, Stein is using his and his staff's street smarts to diversify. He has already acquired a small life insurance company and a New Jersey bank and has come up with an ingenious idea to compete with the hundreds of other mutual funds available today. He established something called the Dreyfus Wall Street Consumer Center, with an 800 number that any customer of numerous collaborating regional banks across the nation can call for advice in picking a fund. The center has been extremely successful in generating business for Dreyfus's forty funds. The day after Sylvia Porter described this free advisory service in her syndicated column, the center's switchboard was inundated with more than three thousand calls. "Timing is the crux of intuition," says Stein.

Examining the Loews Corporation's investment over recent years reveals them to be disconcertingly inconsistent and largely dependent on timing. "We look at each stock on a value basis," says Chairman Laurence Tisch. "We have no preconceived notion of how long we'll hold it. There is a value range for every security. At the bottom end, it becomes interesting. At the top end, it's time to sell." The

Tisch brothers have proved remarkably adept at knowing when to buy and when to sell. In 1985 Loews acquired 12 percent of CBS, a potentially lucrative investment that additionally helped the broadcasting empire to fend off hostile takeovers.

Although intuition often involves responding speedily to an inner impression and not waiting for a weighing-in of all the detailed analysis, there is danger in exploiting a perception too soon. Suspected shifts in the marketplace can turn out to be temporary fads. The raging popularity of computer games, for example, proved to be short-lived, causing dire consequences at Coleco, Atari, and Mattel. Coleco, however, made a remarkable recovery, first with Coleco Vision, which could also play its competitors' games, and then with its Cabbage Patch Kids. The cute, chubby-cheeked dolls were born in the nick of time in 1983, rescuing Coleco from a grievous cash crunch. President Arnold C. Greenberg, who prides himself on knowing when to jump into the unpredictable toy market with a new product, says: "My role is to be the ultimate inspirer, to dream the ultimate dreams, to see the vision, and to impart that vision to others."

Another inspirer and visionary in a similarly fickle industry is Diane Von Furstenberg. She burst onto the fashion scene in the mid-1970s with the simple jersey wrap dresses. This casual but elegant style became the cornerstone of her company and propelled her onto the cover of *Newsweek*. But unfortunately, she has never succeeded in applying her impeccable sense of timing as a style-setter to the marketing end of her business. In fact, the sudden acclaim seemed to send Diane (she addresses everybody by their first name and expects to be called by hers) into a tailspin. "My business got so big, so fast," she recalls.

Faced with an oversupply that landed some of her dresses in bargain basements, she chose to "run rather than cope." In 1978 she licensed her dress business to the giant Puritan Fashions Corporation, while retaining final approval over the designs. A few years later, glimpsing a collection Puritan had put together, she recalls: "I knew they weren't going to work. The clothes were losing their identity. They weren't me anymore." So she terminated her Puritan contract, which had guaranteed her $1 million a year whether the clothes sold or not. Eventually she licensed other companies to make them.

Looking back on the evolution of her business, Diane admits, "Sometimes I was too early with a product. Other times I didn't have the money to launch an advertising program." In both cases, she claims, competitors with greater resources profited from her intuition. "Everything exists in every color and every price," she says, "so your heart has to tell you what to do at any one moment, and whether you're doing it at the right time, with the right people, and with the right backing. Timing is very important, otherwise you'll end up doing the marketing for somebody else who will exploit it."

Occasionally a market is stimulated more by accident than by dream or design. The timing may simply coincide with a change in the national taste. A shift in America's tea-drinking habits, for instance, was wrought by flower children picking herbs in the mountains and packaging them and peddling them in the streets. They inspired the start-up of Celestial Seasonings, a thriving company that began in a barn and was acquired by Kraft in 1984.

A CLASSIC CASE OF BAD TIMING

Without an intuitive sense of timing, a CEO may blindly pursue a venture to disastrous ends. "Distrastrous" hardly describes the tangle of tender offers and PAC-MAN fever that spread through the boardrooms of four of the biggest U.S. corporations in 1982, when Bendix chairman William Agee abortively tried to take over Martin Marietta. Like those once-popular video games in which the object is to eat your enemies before they eat you, first Bendix tried to gobble up Martin Marietta, which in turn responded by trying to swallow Bendix. When it looked like Marietta had bitten off more than it could chew, it invited United Technologies, known for its appetite, to help itself to the leftovers. But before UT could open its mouth, Bendix and Marietta had taken a big chomp out of each other, which you may recall is when Allied Corporation stepped in, devouring Bendix to save it.

Compounding the problems of that ill-timed, ill-conceived takeover attempt was the celebrated romance between Agee and his former chief strategist, Mary Cunningham. Hand in hand (closer than that, newspapers and magazines reported), the pair had divested Bendix of such businesses as forest products and mining, building a cash hoard of half a billion dollars for acquisitions. Mary had also compiled a list of target companies.

But by the time Agee took on Martin Marietta, the propitious moment for such a move had passed. After all, bad timing isn't only doing something at the wrong time, it's failing to perceive that the right time has passed. Conditions had already changed both inside and outside the company. Mary, who had become his wife, was ensconced as a vice president of Joseph E. Seagram, though by Bill's admission, she continued to be his "chief confidante and adviser on all major things at Bendix." Also by Bill's admission, his timing was marred by an important external change: "The stock market started to take off sooner than we expected," jumping the price of Martin Marietta's shares.

THE HOBGOBLIN OF CONSISTENCY

An unintuitive CEO's desire to display consistency can result in terrible timing. "A foolish consistency is the hobgoblin of little minds," Ralph Waldo Emerson wrote. In fact, management studies have shown that CEOs who strive for consistency, instead of intuitively bending, often come a cropper. Conversely, the highest achievers frequently change their priorities, their focus, and even their management style.

Companies, too, become afflicted with the "we've always done it that way" syndrome. Ideas, procedures, and products can become so firmly fixed in management's mind that timing is no longer considered a factor. Or worse yet, gut feelings can congeal in the corporate body so that it is assumed what wouldn't fly one time would automatically crash another. William May, former chairman of American Can Company and later dean of New York University Graduate School of Business, warns that "you have to be alert not to let bad memories masquerade as intuition." He cites his old company's experience with the two-quart milk container, which failed miserably when it was first introduced in 1934. The idea was revived in 1955 in the belief that its time had come. "Our executives turned it down," says May ruefully. Today American Can's competitors have two-quart containers in every dairy case.

American Can's management is presently much more flexible. William Woodside, the current CEO, felt frustrated watching the company's business slowly leak away into its competitors' new containers. "We could see ourselves going downhill," he told *Fortune*. "We had to free up a lot of cash at one time so that we could begin to invest in growing businesses." But his gut feeling to do something big depended on the options available. "You gradually start with the easy stuff and then work up to things that are unthinkable," he said. The company's can business, he realized, wasn't easily salable. On the other hand, the paper division, which constituted a quarter of the company and was more profitable, he finally decided was the most disposable candidate.

After selling off the paper unit, Woodside still hadn't fixed on what to do with the proceeds, when an unexpected opportunity arose to acquire Associated Madison insurance company and its intuitive chief, Gerald Tsai, who is expected to become Woodside's successor. Reviewing these events, what did Woodside have to say about his fortuitous timing? "You sort of ratchet yourself along by having a picture of the future that gradually changes as you learn more facts and add more pieces to it," he explained.

Many business leaders, of course, are instinctively more rigid than Woodside. But according to several management studies, predictably constant business leaders are often accident-prone in today's volatile economy. They tend to live by pronouncements like "maximum two weeks' inventory," "no overtime," and "promote from within"—as if policies that work one time will work just as well another. They confuse a feverish work pace with high accomplishment. They respond slowly to changing conditions, often failing to take remedial action for a long time after spotting a problem. For example, they tolerate ineffective subordinates, hoping their performance will somehow improve. In general, they shy away from verve and boldness but are usually too arrogant to seek advice.

"Rigidity of procedure is something I understand," says Helen Gurley Brown, editor of *Cosmopolitan*. "After twenty years at *Cosmo* I catch myself saying, 'We've always done it this way.' I know the instant the words are out of my mouth that it's wrong. But *Cosmo* has been such a success you tend to get a little high and mighty, even though that way lies unsuccess."

An intuitive leader who has reaped high profits for the Hearst Corporation by keeping the changing aspirations of the "Cosmo girl" clearly in mind, Brown has nevertheless laid down certain editorial dictums that she refuses to depart from. "We've never run pro and con pieces about any subject in the same issue," she says. But then she adds: "The minute I say 'never' I think I'm a complete jerk. After all, change is the only thing any of us can count on."

Brown admits to making weekly visits to a psychiatrist to help her find a fresh approach for solving office problems. As a boss, she also confesses to feeling up some days and down others. "All of us have our moods," she says. "But being mercurial around an office is a little alarming. You have to keep a fairly even keel in dealing with the people you work with." She considers timing of key importance in knowing when and when not to discuss a problem with an employee. "If you've just turned down a raise request, you better postpone any other bad news for that person."

Psychologists who study office behavior report that some of the most successful bosses seem to place less value on consistency than does editor Brown. They are close to their

staff one day and distant the next. They communicate orally
with some colleagues and in writing with others. Sometimes
they analyze interminably, other times they move abruptly.
They can be big talkers or good listeners, depending on the
occasion. In other words, their management style is changing constantly. But they are consistently good at sizing up
different situations and people. And their timing is often
phenomenal.

13

CONFIRMATION FROM THE HALLS OF ACADEMIA AND SCIENCE

THERE is no perfect validation of an inner experience. Nevertheless, a number of scientists, psychologists, and academicians are trying hard to prove the importance of hunches in business. The specialists engaged in this work don't all agree, and they have difficulty establishing the bottom-line value of intuition. But in one way or another they have come up with evidence that: (1) the intuitive executive is effective; (2) his or her chief ally is confidence in the nebulous process by which innovations and solutions can leap fully conceived from the subconscious; and (3) the implacable enemies of intuition in the executive suite are those left-brained, B-school-trained, analysis-happy, computer-oriented mercenaries, who also march under the banner of "consultant."

Consultants, it is sometimes said, have the kind of mind that wonders if what works well in practice will stand up in theory. In the preceding chapters we heard sufficient evidence from CEOs on how intuition helped them, to know that it works in practice. In this chapter, adopting the mentality of the consultant, we will glance back at some of the experiments performed to test the validity of various intuition theories.

PROPHETS AND PROFITS

Two pioneers investigating the bottom-line impact of intuition on business were the parapsychologist E. Douglas Dean and engineer John Mihalasky, an industrial management professor at the New Jersey Institute of Technology. This duo spent more than a decade at the institute testing chief executives' precognitive power and the correlation between this ability and the profitability of their companies. The book *Executive ESP,* published in 1974, chronicled Dean and Mihalasky's findings. "I think we'll learn a lot more about intuition as science keeps progressing," Mihalasky says today. "Many of the things that are now being claimed, we were saying fifteen years ago."

One of their tests involved asking executives to predict a 100-digit number that was then randomly selected by computer anytime from two hours to two years later. From this exercise it was discovered that the most effective executives frequently have superior extrasensory perception. More than 80 percent of CEOs who had doubled their company's profits within a five-year period proved to have above-average precognitive powers. The high scorers were also found to be dynamic, hurry-up bosses, while the low scorers were more mañana types.

Mihalasky visualizes precognition as a flow of information particles moving forward and backward in time. "Physicists have been telling us for years that information is matter and that time is a continuum," he explains. "It's only man that divides perpetuity into yesterday, today, and tomorrow. So if you look at information this way, it's something that is continuously available. The question is, how do we get it?"

The professor uses the stock market crash of 1929 to illustrate his point that this information flow can actually be tapped. For precognitive investors, he claims, there was strong evidence that the crash was coming and that there would be violent repercussions. "But today we tend to dismiss their 'I told you sos' as Monday-morning quarterbacking." Cautions Mihalasky, "If something goes beyond the logic that we understand, we say 'Forget it.'"

Mihalasky is still carrying on related experiments but is presently concentrating on what he calls the "dominance factor" in intuition. "Whoever controls the group can impede the intuition of the other members," he explains.

"This dominance can take the form of male superiority, white superiority, or even father-in-law superiority. An intuitive decision-maker will score poorly in precognitive tests if he or she is controlled by somebody else."

Although Mihalasky visualizes a world populated by both "psi-hitters" and "psi-missers," he, like Dr. Eugene Gendlin (see Chapter 8), offers certain recommendations for inducing intuition:

1. Concentrate on what is unique about the problem. Intuitive flashes don't occur when you are disconnected. They come on a need-to-know basis when you are immersed in a situation.

2. Be aware of the gaps in your knowledge. Immersed in a situation, the mind begins to see what information is missing or becomes skeptical of that which it has. Only then does the subconscious reach out for something new.

3. Make connections between diverse factors. Your mind will automatically do the synthesizing for you. If subordinates do the synthesizing and give you a summary, it may be incorrect.

4. Avoid becoming overloaded with information. With too much data ("and this," said Mihalasky, "is an ever present threat in our computer age"), the conscious mind interferes with the subconscious. Then even if you get a flash, the rational system is likely to destroy the "intuitive component."

Another attempt to link intuition with business effectiveness was made by Professor Weston Agor of the University of Texas at El Paso, who was mentioned in Chapter 7. Between 1981 and 1982 Agor conducted a nationwide survey of two thousand managers in business, government, and academia.

His raw data were obtained from twenty-seven multiple-choice questions. This ten-minute quiz was based largely on a questionnaire called the Myers-Briggs Type Indicator, which has been used by psychologists for many years to measure personality differences as well as intuitive ability. A few sample questions from Agor's test:

I work best at (a) improving something, (b) inventing something, (c) both improving and inventing.

I usually solve problems (a) logically and rationally, (b) according to my feelings, (c) with both logic and feelings equally.

When I'm reading about something new, I'm most likely to remember (a) the main ideas, (b) facts and details, (c) both the main ideas and details.

Would you rather have as a friend someone who (a) is always coming up with new ideas? (b) has both feet on the ground?

A complicated tabulation system determines a manager's "ability" and also "potential ability" to use intuition. (To the four questions above, an intuitive person would answer *b, b, a,* and *a.*) The test results formed the basis for Agor's textbook *Intuitive Management: Integrating Left and Right Brain Skills.* The answers revealed that top-level leaders rely more on intuition than managers lower in the organization. Also, woman managers consistently scored higher than men in their reliance on intuition, and Asians higher than Occidentals. But the women were more reluctant to admit using intuition, fearing that it would be viewed as a sign of weakness.

In 1984 Agor conducted a follow-up study of the top 10 percent of the scorers to try to obtain a more complete picture of how these executives use their intuition. This time he designed a more probing exam consisting of eleven open-ended questions, which could be administered either by mail or by interview. Asked for were specific decisions based primarily on intuition, and particular techniques these top scorers might have developed to enhance their intuitive powers. The executives were also asked if they kept their reliance on intuition a secret. All but one of the seventy respondents acknowledged using intuition in making their most important decisions, though many did not reveal this fact to their associates. Said one: "I don't think intuition is some magical thing. I think it is a subconscious drawing from innumerable experiences which are stored. You draw from this reserve without conscious thought."

The situations identified as most conducive to using intuition were those involving a high degree of risk or uncertainty, and problems with little precedent but with several plausible solutions. Asked how they knew which alternative to pursue, the executives variously described: "a growing excitement in the pit of my stomach," "a feeling of total harmony," "a total sense of commitment," and "a burst of enthusiasm and energy." Said one, "It feels like a bolt of lightning or sudden flash that this is the solution." At the same time, many of the respondents admitted that their worst decisions stemmed from not heeding their intuition. "I have had situations," said one, "where I failed to follow up on a feeling that things weren't right, and made a decision which really screwed things up."

There are a number of organizations attempting to both verify intuition and find new applications for it. The Mobius Society in Los Angeles is engaged in a research project called PSI-Q, attempting to identify highly intuitive individuals in various occupations. SRI International in Menlo Park, California, is the experimental lab of physicists Russell Targ and Harold Puthoff, America's indefatigable ESP testers and authors. The McDonnell Laboratory for Psychical Research in St. Louis has been conducting what it calls "pathological phenomenon studies of hauntings and poltergeists." It was founded by the late aircraft manufacturer James Smith McDonnell, who believed in the occult (Phantom and Voodoo were the names given to two of his company's jet fighters) and hoped to contact dead test pilots. The Institute of Noetic Sciences in Sausalito, California, founded by former astronaut Edgar Mitchell, is currently trying to bring Soviet cosmonauts and American astronauts together in a "a nonpolitical way" to apply their combined intuition to the solution of world problems.

It's a little disconcerting to sit in Mitchell's office in Jupiter, Florida, looking out at the yachts parading up and down the Intracoastal Waterway, and at the wildlife preserve on the far bank, and listen to him recite the world's woes: "Exhaustion of natural resources; the growing tension between rich and poor; the threat of nuclear destruction; coexistence of unemployment and inflation; hazardous substances in food, air, and water; the ungovernability of the cities . . ." His inventory of the earth's ills rolls on and on.

"These problems prove that technology has outstripped our ability to make society work," he says, pausing to catch his breath. But this scientist back from outer space believes that the only way to correct our earthly problems is by "reaching higher intuitive centers of the mind." This, of course, is what Eastern mystics have been telling us for centuries.

Matina Horner, the president of Radcliffe College, who holds a PhD in psychology, agrees. "You can't solve many of today's problems by straight linear thinking," she says. "It takes leaps of faith to sense the connections that are not necessarily obvious." This she thinks will be a vitally important future role of intuition. "As an educator and scholar," she adds, "I have to believe that we will find out a lot more about what intuition is and how it works. Otherwise, few of our problems will ever be understood or solved."

One of Horner's main psychological interests has been the so-called fear-of-success syndrome affecting women. She has studied and written about this subject. Before becoming president in 1972, she tested groups of university women and discovered that 75 percent showed fear of success, which she says is a "learned phenomenon," but based on "negative intuition." Radcliffe students, she noted, "are chosen primarily because of their high ability, achievement, and motivation." Yet many didn't follow their instincts and purposely "changed their plans toward a less ambitious, more traditionally feminine direction, fearing the negative consequences of success."

It is when she herself fails to follow her intuition, Horner admits, that she is most error-prone. "When I've had an intuitive response and haven't followed it, saying, 'Look, you don't have any logical explanation for this,' I've been wrong. Particularly in hiring, when everything on paper is perfect, all the recommendations are terrific, and I don't follow my intuition, I've regretted it."

Horner believes there may be important sex differences between right- and left-hemisphere use. " A very efficient kind of information processing is probably available to those who have highly developed right hemispheres that somehow interconnect with logic," she says. "Having been trained in chemistry and math, and then moving into psychology, where the questions are more elusive, I've had to deal with this intuitiveness. Even administratively I've come to respect it, though I don't call it intuition because that word doesn't hold up very well at a board of trustees meeting."

MORE CHEMICAL THAN MYSTICAL

The Eureka factor remains an elusive, hard-to-grasp, seemingly mystical power. Even talking about intuition still makes some executives squirm. As Matina Horner admits, it is too amorphous a feeling to reveal to hardheaded policymakers. Yet recent brain research provides tangible proof that it's possibly more chemical than mystical. Processes within our brain trigger the release of certain hormones that affect the way we think and can even change our bodies.

By implanting electrodes in the brain's cortex, neuroscientists are able to study how various signals are processed across an array of neurons. These researchers are becoming convinced that thoughts and feelings, including intuitive flashes, are produced by chemical and electrical activity in the network of nerve cells composing the brain. They are confident that they soon will be able to create a new portrait of the mind based on these experiments. So verification of the whole intuitive process may be about to veer off in an entirely different direction.

There are several current theories about how these pathways into the mind are opened up. Scientists subscribing to the so-called switchboard theory believe that the 10 billion neurons composing man's brain arrange themselves into interconnected electrochemical circuits called engrams. The neurologists have also concluded that unconscious memory employs separate brain circuits from those used in conscious recall. But in both circuits the engram is pictured as thought's pathway. Like the individual light bulbs in those moving signs that spell out late-news headlines across the front of a building, each neuron may be turning on and off in an infinite number of engrams. The problem is nobody has ever seen an engram.

A radically different view of the thought path is offered by Dr. E. Roy John, director of the brain research laboratories at New York University Medical Center. Dr. John does not envision thought or memory as interconnected circuitry but as "coherent temporal patterns" of resonating neurons. According to his theory, the neurons act in "ensembles," not as individual units. "The brain is a big democracy," he says. "It doesn't listen to a single voice." As for his frustrated fellow scientists searching for an engram, he thinks they're looking for the wrong thing. "Instead of a groove, they should be looking for a wave. The engram is like a radio signal. Even though you can't see it, you can pick it up on your receiver."

The brain's myriad neurons, however, have been seen and studied for years. Each neuron consists of a nucleus, an axon that serves as the cell's transmitter, and a number of receiving antennae called dendrites. The gaps between the neurons are known as synapses. And it is the molecular action at the synapse, when one neuron fires and its chemical signal is picked up by neighboring neurons on the other side of the gap, that intrigues scientists. They see this action at the synapse gap as holding the secret to memory and to thought storage and transmission. Anatomically, it may be the place in the brain where the intuitive flash occurs and the Eureka factor comes into play.

Can anything be done to improve transmission and reception in the brain's cells? Mind-expanding drugs like LSD receive a great deal of attention these days. Contrary to common belief, amphetamines curtail brain-cell transmission. But various brain chemicals have been identified that tend to make us feel shy or aggressive, confident or fearful, happy or depressed—moods that affect our intuition. They can also affect the strength of our all-important immune system, determining our ability to fight off disease. Cancer patients are now taught by some biofeedback specialists to relax deeply and visualize their white blood cells as "valiant white knights" or as "overpowering polar bears" tearing apart the cancer cells. One statistical study has shown that terminal patients using this thought process live twice as long after the diagnosis of cancer as those who do not.

"Food for thought," is an old expression that is taking on new meaning. Dietary experts now believe that certain edibles, especially eggs, soybeans, and liver, are absorbed directly from the bloodstream by the brain. There they are converted into acetylcholine, a chemical transmitter that carries nerve impulses across the synapse. Nobody is suggesting that eating a hefty four-egg omelette every morning will stimulate intuition. But diet does probably play a role in memory improvement.

Alcohol, on the other hand, tends to shrink the brain by interfering with its ability to make proteins, the building blocks of the neurons. Although neurons cannot reproduce themselves (a loss of brain tissue through illness or injury is permanent), their protein content is constantly forming and disappearing. Man in effect grows a new brain every month, but with the same neurons and engrams, just as the remake of an LP record has the same grooves and squiggles and plays the same old tune.

So what the artists, philosophers, and spiritual leaders have been telling us through the ages is now being confirmed by the neuroscientists, who say: "Yes, there is a quantifiable chemical link between mind and matter, spirit and body, imagination and reality."

OR IS IT COSMOLOGICAL?

Immunologist Jonas Salk is so convinced of intuition's power that he is now devoting himself totally to uncovering its riddles. And with the same intensity that he once applied to solving the mysteries of polio. "Intuition is a word that bespeaks a certain structure," he says. "We haven't identified that structure yet. But contained in it is the same essence contained in genetic material." He sees the learning-from-within aspect of intuition as an automatic response similar to procreativity. "It's part of a continuum," he says.

Today, Salk is distilling thousands of pages of notes he has compiled for a new book on intuition and creativity. He believes that intuition will eventually be understood and viewed as a natural phenomenon. "But this will happen slowly," he says, "the way the theory of relativity was gradually understood. First we have to see ourselves in relation to the cosmos." He feels intensely the importance of making intuition and creativity understandable in cosmological terms rather than in mystical terms. "The subject has seized me," he admits. "I'm trying to bring it all together and make it legitimate by making it scientific."

THE LESSONS OF BIOFEEDBACK

A number of researchers studying how the intuitive mind works believe that the best understanding of the Eureka factor will emerge from brain scans and biofeedback. The realization that humans can regulate most body functions and alleviate pain by becoming sensitive to subtle internal signals and then *feeding back* this information to the controlling organs is being greeted as a new discovery in the Western hemisphere. However, Yogis practicing self-regulation and sensory deprivation have for thousands of years been performing all sorts of "miracles," from walking barefoot on burning coals to being buried alive. It is by restricting sensory input that Yogis are also able to intensify their awareness. "By becoming blind," they say, "we are able to see more clearly."

In the same way, biofeedback is being studied as a means of enhancing intuitive seeing. The husband-and-wife team of Alyce and Elmer Green at Topeka's Menninger Foundation are among the most experienced biofeedback specialists in the country. They have been working with patients there for many years, attempting to pinpoint the moment of discovery. The two most fertile periods, they have found, come during the so-called hypnagogic state just before drifting off to sleep and during the hypnapompic state while in the process of awakening. "At these two times, while in sort of a no-man's-land between being asleep and awake," says Alyce Green, "the conscious and unconscious minds are in closest touch." She prefers the term "unconscious" over "subconscious," claiming that "Freud gave 'subconscious' a bad name" because he associated it so often with selfishness and greed. In addition, she says: "'Unconscious' also includes the 'superconscious,' a higher state of consciousness that one gets in touch with sometimes." Superconsciousness is perhaps yet another way of describing the Eureka factor.

The Greens have concluded that it's also possible to get into that state through deep relaxation or meditation, inducing the hypnagogic state the way Zen Buddhists do. The body, mind, and emotions must be shifted into a quiet state, yet the mind must be receptive and alert. "Then," says Alyce Green, "it's possible to program your unconscious, because what you *vividly* visualize in that state tends to come into being. But first you must ask your mind to give answers. Then you must *believe* that they will come to you." Those answers, she explains, don't have to be visual. They can be auditory. "Anything seen or heard in this state of reverie is considered hypnagogic imagery."

However, she feels that too often people aren't aware of what comes to them intuitively. She recommends quickly writing down ideas that surface just before dropping off to sleep or while emerging from a deep sleep. "We let so much brush by without even looking at it," she says. "After we get these ideas, they have to be consciously examined again and again. Otherwise, like dreams, they simply vanish."

Many creative people, she points out, have described states of "near-dream reverie" in which inspirational ideas suddenly appeared. Robert Louis Stevenson was able to

conjure plots by commanding what he called "the brown-
ies" of his mind to furnish him with a story. German
chemist Friedrich August Kekule, who developed the ring
theory, told of a series of deep reveries during which atoms
"gamboled" before his eyes. They were "turning and
twisting in snakelike motion," he said, "when one of the
snakes had seized hold of his own tail." Thus Kekule
conceived the revolutionary idea that some organic com-
pounds occur in closed chains, or rings.

The Greens believe too much stress has been placed on
left- and right-brain specialization. "You know there was a
big to-do about the two hemispheres and how never the
twain shall meet," says Alyce Green. "This, of course, is
not true. The two sides of the brain are connected and they
work back and forth, even if they do perform different
functions."

Dedicated to the concept of right- and left-brain interde-
pendence, neurologists, too, are attempting to confirm the
importance of harmony inside the head. They are using both
the EEG (electroencephalograph) and the PET (positron
emission tomography) scan, by which a picture of the brain
is taken after injection of a radioactive isotope into the
bloodstream, to measure activity in the two hemispheres.
Balanced activity has been observed during periods of
meditation. This has led the neuroscientists to declare that
harmony of the two hemispheres appears to be the outstanding characteristic of deep states of consciousness.

One brain researcher showed films to volunteers using
special lenses that allowed them to view things with either
the right or left hemisphere. Described by Carl Sagan in his
book *The Dragons of Eden*, this experiment indicated "a
remarkable tendency for the right hemisphere—despite its
imaginative, synthesizing power—to view the world as
more unpleasant, hostile, and even disgusting. This nega-
tivism," Sagan says, "is apparently strongly tempered in
everyday life by the more easygoing left hemisphere."
Asian mystics, of course, have for thousands of years
stressed the need for inner harmony as the unity of yin and

yang, consciousness and unconsciousness, mind and body, man and woman, and heaven and earth.

But intuition, whether it comes primarily from the right side of the brain or from the two sides harmonizing with the full-bodied sound of a pair of stereo speakers, somehow enables us to bend reality to our will. We see things the way we want to, positively or negatively, traditionally or innovatively. "Feedforward" is the term Stanford neurophysiologist Karl Pribram uses to describe those images of achievement that spur us on to creative action. A mental image triggers the same neural connections in the autonomic nervous system as an actual experience, and research has shown that the body can't distinguish between the two. That's why a vivid mental picture of ultimate success helps steer an individual intuitively to a desired objective.

V

VERIFICATION

14

LISTEN FOR THOSE WARNING BELLS

WISHFUL thinking is not intuition. Yet it's easy to confuse hope with a hunch. William Agee, as we saw, may have confused his desire to acquire Martin Marietta with the notion that its management would see the synergy of merging with Bendix and surrender. As psychologists warn, "Failure to maintain some degree of pessimism is to be in a state of peril." So don't disregard those nagging voices trying to tell you what you don't want to hear. They may come bearing a career-saving message.

No one is immune to failure. Even the most intuitive executives can cite examples of when they allowed positive hunches to carry them away in the face of a negative forecast—and to a sorry end.

Admittedly, a conflict can arise between the trust it takes to pursue an intuitive flash and the skepticism needed to spurn a flash-in-the-pan idea. At first the two kinds of flashes may seem equally alluring. So listen for the warning bell before you shout, "Eureka!"

There is no faking the Eureka factor. Gut feelings have to be genuine or they aren't worth listening to. However, born losers with an overwhelming need to prove their own brilliance may not know the difference. "Look, I've got this feeling," they'll say, shooting from the hip rather than from the head. Headhunters are frank to admit that the overriding fear in hiring a new CEO today is that he'll turn out to be a hipshooter.

Professor Eugene Jennings of the Michigan State University Business School, author of *Executive Success*, claims to have found the two most common traits of the failure-prone business leader: the "illusion of mastery of all life's events" and the "illusion of immunity to bad luck." Operating in concert, those two misconceptions are an obvious duet of disaster.

Jennings has been collecting data since 1969 on success and failure at the corporate pinnacle, particularly keeping tabs on the business life expectancy of chief executive officers and chief operating officers. He reports that today about 25 percent of the two top officers either resign or are fired before reaching retirement age, compared with 5 percent in 1969. "Disagreement over where the company is going and how it should get there," he believes, precipitates many of the early departures. "The conflict is not merely a clash of wills, but a clash of intuition as well," he says.

Almost a third of those CEOs and COOs leaving early, according to Jennings, get caught up in some kind of palace revolt—evidence that ambition or instinct or both lead them astray. But then, today's fast track is known for its dangerous hairpin turns, requiring the hard-driving executive to use superb timing and intuition, along with the usual operating skills. Remember, even the most far-out new idea can be tested against a number of practical criteria.

DO THE FACTS SUPPORT YOUR HUNCH?

A good question to ask yourself in trying to decide whether to trust a hunch is: Do facts exist that could perhaps eliminate some of the uncertainty? This is the time to switch on the computers and to let the number-crunchers loose to check on costs and return on investment. Yes, at this stage even the consultants, investment bankers, and market surveyors can be called in for a look-see, as long as they aren't allowed to douse the creative fires.

Gathering facts about the personalities involved in a business gamble is important too. In the case of Bendix's assault on Martin Marietta, one miscalculation admitted later by Agee was the intransigence of opposing CEO Tom

Pownall. Anybody in the aerospace business could have told Agee that the former navy officer would never give up the ship. What's more, they could have assured Agee that Pownall would stick to his threat and counterattack by buying Bendix's stock.

BE PREPARED TO BACK DOWN

Agee could have called off his attack right up until literally the witching hour of midnight when he began buying Martin Marietta stock. Why, then, did he blindly pursue his quarry, destroying Bendix and wrecking his credibility as a CEO? Several books, including one by his wife, Mary, fail to answer that question satisfactorily. One thing is clear. Neither Bill nor Mary—both products of the Harvard Business School—put much faith in their intuition. At the same time, they spurned the advice of Salomon Brothers, Bendix's original investment bankers, as well as the advice of a number of Bendix directors, who urged Agee to back down before it was too late. But Agee totally misjudged the final outcome. "There will be no dismemberment of Bendix," he proclaimed.

REHEARSE YOUR IDEA
WITH A CORE OF ADVISERS

Repetition in one's mind of the original business objective seems to bolster an intuitive spark. Psychiatrist Abraham Zaleznik, who teaches leadership at the Harvard Business School, explains that continual rehearsing is a crucial part of the verification process. "It becomes a ritual for instinctive business leaders," he says.

Christie Ann Hefner, president and "hare apparent," according to her father, Hugh, the founder of Playboy Enterprises, keeps rehearsing her ideas with a small high-level group. "I try to get them to challenge my hypotheses," says the willowy brunette. Aware that her father supplied the creative genius, she has purposely developed complementary strengths. "Now I am the person managing and leading and making the decisions," she says. "But I can't rely entirely on my own intuition. So I have surrounded myself with a lot of talent."

Joseph McKinney, the Tyler Corporation's intuitive CEO, never lets himself or his fellow officers forget their fallibility. Having gone belly-up in a previous corporate incarnation, he remembers painfully that the most innovative plans sometimes flop. Although Tyler is prospering, he still conducts "stray-bullet drills," as he calls them, "to make sure we can identify all the unlikely bad news." For the same reason he prefers to hire executives who have similarly suffered business reversals. "Bloody noses are great teachers," he says.

Ralph Bahna, president and managing director of the Cunard Line, conducts rehearsals all the time in front of his inner circle of executives. "I'll get a gut feeling and start talking about it," he says. "That way omissions and gaps come to mind. Sometimes it triggers a much bigger idea, or one of the other guys will turn it around and say: 'Hey, fantastic, but why don't we do it this way?' "

He cites the example of the trouble Cunard was having selling Alaska cruises on the *Sagafjord*, a top-rated cruise ship. Another ship, the *Cunard Princess*, was doing very well on the same run. "It's an awareness problem," Bahna kept telling his staff. One of the other executives mentioned that most of the travel agents in the Northwest were young women. "Why don't we give them a free fur coat if they sell a cruise?" he suggested. *Sagafjord* sales picked up immediately.

LISTEN TO THE RUMBLINGS FROM BELOW

Isolation at the top is a well-known hazard facing chief executives. Subordinates hesitate to knock on the CEO's door, especially if it means being a bearer of bad news. No matter how intuitive they are, smart CEOs keep an ear cocked for what the grapevine in their company is saying. As Professor Jennings points out, the "illusion of immunity to bad luck" can plague a CEO. But sensing the mood of an organization, and slyly tapping the collective intuition of the rest of the employees, can reduce a CEO's chance of being unlucky.

Who will be lucky as a leader and who won't be? Professor Jennings calls this the "greatest guessing game in business." He says that it has always been a gamble how a CEO will fare and that it always will be, "because there's no rung on the way up the corporate ladder that prepares you for the top one."

Men who made their mark as inventors down in the shop sometimes have trouble getting used to the polish of the executive suite. The hip-shooting, gut-feeling entrepreneur, in particular, can find it pretty nerve-frazzling trying to comprehend the subtle chemistry of his own company once it has passed beyond the start-up stage. Edwin Land, for instance, ran Polaroid for the first dozen or so years. When it started growing too fast, he wisely put in place a top management team headed by Tom Wyman, now the CBS chairman, to handle day-to-day operations, and Land stayed in the lab directing research.

Ray Kroc, McDonald's intuitive impresario, remained president until he died. But he sensibly installed a management team to take charge of the Golden Arches and appointed himself the company's "marketing conscience." In that capacity he inspected stores and chatted with customers, relying on his well-tested ability to catch the vibes of the fast-food industry he created.

A number of other founders, like Armand Hammer, Occidental Petroleum's octogenarian chairman, never relax their grip on the company controls. Hammer was trained as a medical doctor. But an intuitive deal-making streak took him into the oil business, and he remains today one of that industry's most incorrigible hunchplayers, who is still predicting that oil will hit $100 a barrel before the end of the decade.

Ever questing for new deals, new friends, and new art acquisitions—he picked up Leonardo da Vinci's *Codex Leicester* for $5.2 million in 1979—the good doctor still cavorts around the globe in his Boeing 727 with "1-Oxy" emblazoned on the tail. The plane is outfitted with an office, a master bedroom, three telephones, and in case the aging chairman suffers a heart attack aloft, a cardiac defibrillator. But Hammer does not have a weak heart when it comes to gambling. In 1982 he played his biggest hunch and completed what was then the largest U.S. oil merger ever: the $4 billion takeover of Cities Service.

Hammer still says, "It's the best deal I ever made." But Wall Street analysts claim Oxy is "choking on debt" trying to swallow the domestic oil giant. Since then, struggling for solvency, Hammer has fired a whole string of presidents and suffered a falling-out with Oxy's former number-one stockholder, David Murdock, a takeover genius himself, who boasts of practicing "brain calisthenics." A number of departed Oxy executives think Hammer won't listen anymore, and that his legendary intuition has finally led him astray.

STAY TUNED TO YOUR INTUITION

What kind of brain calisthenics does it take to stay tuned in at the top? Just realizing that the mind screens out what it doesn't want to hear is part of the answer. We all know how easy it is to dismiss ideas that don't fit our preconceived notions. Well, it's just as easy to dismiss those nagging voices and queasy sensations accompanying hunches that aren't sitting very well.

The obvious solution is to come up with an intuitive alternative. But that's hard. A hunch being adhered to may be firmly rooted, despite the discomfort it is causing. Dr. Eugene Gendlin, the University of Chicago psychologist who developed the technique called focusing for inducing intuition, has also devised a system for dislodging bum steers. Advised Gendlin: "You should say to yourself as if it were true, 'This decision feels fine. The problem is solved, and I feel good about it, don't I?' If you pay attention to your body, you will almost immediately feel a very distinct sense of discomfort."

The next step is to keep reexamining this discomfort,

even though you don't know what's causing it. You should search for a single word that epitomizes the problem. "Then wait to hear from your body," he says. If that word doesn't feel right, you pick another, and then another, until you finally hit the right word. "Now," says Gendlin, "you see the whole scene more clearly, and you feel a physical change in your body. The lump comes undone." He equates this sensation with a sort of "instant hindsight." Some CEOs, of course, may think that's hogwash, particularly founders who launched large enterprises on a gut feeling. Understandably, they may believe their intuition is infallible.

Just as intuition can be sharpened and tested with psychological coaching, the verification process can be improved with practice. Here again the psychologists offer some suggestions. CEOs, they say, should consider keeping a record of their important insights and the proven accuracy of these ideas. Knowing that your batting average is good builds confidence in future hunches.

CAN THE IDEA BE TEST-MARKETED?

Business surveys, unlike the polling done for political candidates, are aimed more at preventing failure than assuring success. But quite often it's possible for CEOs to order up a statistical reconnaissance of the marketplace they are using their intuition to exploit. As one of them says: "We try to put the chart before the course."

Verification of intuition about the marketplace is carried on Star Wars–style these days. Visit the CRT room of Audits & Surveys Inc. in New York City at almost any hour of the day or night and you'll find thirty or more living robots plugged into an automated opinion-gathering system called CATI (Computer Assisted Telephone Interviewing) that is verifying the preferences and prejudices of men, women, and children about everything from a ride on a wide-bodied plane to Coca-Cola's megabrand strategy. A&S conducts more than 2.5 million of these CATI calls a year.

Preprogrammed, randomly selected questions for the surveyors to ask appear magically on the CRT screens. And the tabulated results of the answers can be summoned instantaneously with the punch of a computer key. About the only human element left in this superscientific verification system is the interviewer's voice. Even that is being replaced by speech synthesizers.

Solomon Dutka, the former atomic physicist who founded and runs A&S, points to a major difference between verifying intuition in science and business. "The setting and testing of hypotheses goes on in both fields," he says. "But the hypothesis that is proven in business turns out to be true only for a short time. There ain't no constants in business because people keep changing. Pretty soon you've got to test your hypothesis all over again."

GIVE YOUR IDEAS TIME TO RIPEN

Cunard's President Bahna explains that when the *QE-II* returned to its transatlantic run after doing a stint as a troopship during the Falkland Islands affair, passenger sales were poor. He was bitterly embroiled in restitution claims against the British government. But the idea suddenly struck him to combine the sale of a *QE-II* ticket to Europe with a free Concorde flight home. "The concept was aimed at executives who didn't have time to sail round-trip," he explains.

Cunard promptly test-marketed the idea, but it bombed. Bahna was baffled and kept telling his associates that Cunard hadn't allowed enough time for the idea to catch on. "Next year we really rolled the dice," he says, "and chartered ten thousand Concorde seats. It was a great financial success." Now Cunard links the *QE-II* trip to Concorde flights all over the world. "The idea's dynamite," says Bahna.

THE PROOF IS IN THE PRODUCT

In today's unpredictable business environment, it's hard to tell whether even the best hunches will sell. A CEO may come up with an ingenious idea that the board of directors buys but that the public won't accept. Howard Stein, for instance, launched a "moral" mutual fund at Dreyfus composed only of companies that complied strictly with environmental safeguards and fair employment practices. It was the first such fund specifically designed to appeal to universities and nonprofit foundations. "Ironically, this Third Century Fund has outperformed many others," reports Stein, "but the colleges called it a 'do-good attempt' and stuck to traditional investments." The logic behind Stein's concept did not make it succeed.

At the same time, an ingenious new idea that doesn't survive a logical assault isn't necessarily wrong. When Robert Goddard suggested rocket propulsion as the only feasible power source for space travel, critics quite logically, it seemed, scorned the idea, insisting there isn't anything in space for the rocket to push against. But rockets, we know now, work because the momentum of the hot gases rushing backward is matched by the forward momentum of the rocket's shell.

In Goddard's mind the rocket propulsion idea had already survived an internal screening. Even though he couldn't explain exactly why it would work, he could visualize the rocket successfully soaring off into space. Psychologists don't know precisely how this mental screening is carried out. But a subconscious process goes on that constantly weighs new ideas against the mind's accumulated wisdom.

Final verification of intuition's power comes with the new product or concept. But this tangible proof that the Eureka factor works does not depict the sloppy process of discovery. Gazing upon a sparkling new creation, it's impossible to untangle the pieces put together by the original perception, or to tell precisely how or in what order they were assembled. The chances are that development took a haphazard, zigzag course. After percolating in the originator's mind, the separate elements suddenly synthesized into a vision that could not have been predicted. All of the analysis, all of the forecasting, all of the extrapolation from past and current experience could only have provided a sense of feasibility. It was an unrelenting, indefinable inner urge that told the originator to keep on trying.

The extraordinary career of Chester Carlson, the inventor of xerography, illustrates all of these points. Late in life, Carlson and his wife became fascinated with ESP. It was he who funded the precognition experiments conducted by Douglas Dean and John Mihalasky at the New Jersey Institute of Technology.

The son of an itinerant barber, Carlson showed early interest in both chemistry and the graphic arts. In high school he pursued the two fields at once by picking up a discarded printing press and launching a little magazine for amateur chemists. After obtaining a degree in physics from Caltech, he was hired by Bell Labs in New York City. But those were Depression days, and he was soon laid off. Luckily he landed another job with an electrical firm. Attending law school at night, he was put in charge of the company's patents.

Two things quickly became apparent to Carlson. There were never enough carbon copies of the patent specifications around the office. All offices, he decided, needed a machine that could quickly duplicate documents. Just married, he also felt he wasn't getting ahead fast enough.

"I though the possibility of making an invention might kill two birds with one stone," Carlson said. "It would be a chance to do the world some good and also a chance to do myself some good." At the same time, he was aware of two natural phenomena that might have a bearing on the kind of invention he had in mind: materials of opposite electrical charges are attracted to each other; and certain materials became better conductors of electricity when exposed to light.

Reflecting on early writings about photoconductivity, Carlson later said, "Things don't come to mind readily but all of a sudden, like pulling things out of the air. You have to get your inspiration somewhere, and usually you get it from reading something else."

He began rudimentary experiments in the kitchen of his apartment, then set up a small lab and hired a refugee

German physicist to help him. It was above a saloon in Astoria, Queens, that the Xerox process was born on October 22, 1938. But during the next five years more than twenty companies spurned Carlson's invention, refusing to help him develop it. "Some were indifferent," he recalled. "Several expressed mild interest, and one or two were antagonistic. How difficult it was to convince anyone that my tiny plates and rough image held the key to a tremendous new industry."

Finally, in 1944, Battelle Memorial Institute, a nonprofit research organization in Columbus, Ohio, signed a royalty-sharing contract with Carlson and began developing the process. Three years later Battelle found a small photo-paper firm called Haloid that would produce a xerographic machine. It wasn't until 1959 that the first practical office copier was unveiled. Able to make copies on plain paper at the touch of a button, it was an instant success.

The Haloid Company evolved into the Xerox Corporation in 1961. Its stock became a hot issue even for those go-go years. So frantically did Xerox try to keep pace with demand that in 1963 every third employee had been hired that year. In the town of Webster, New York, ten miles east of Rochester, a sprawling research and manufacturing complex blossomed on a thousand acres where only apple trees had grown.

The giant corporation has never forgotten the lessons taught by Chester Carlson, who died in 1968. "From this life, we of Xerox have learned much," said Joseph C. Wilson, Haloid's president and the man who gambled on xerography. "First, we will never forget that the individual is the origin of the great creative act. Second, we learned that great rewards come to those who see needs that have not been clearly identified by others, and who have the innovating capacity to devise products and services which fill these needs."

15

PICKING THE RIGHT-BRAINED BOSS

THE higher up an executive moves, the more often he or she will be forced into making intuitive, long-range, nonlogical decisions. However, there is widespread suspicion in business against decisions that stem from personality. And since visions of the future are distinctly personal, they can trigger conflicts within an organization. To build a following while embarking on a new concept takes a charismatic leader.

How are such leaders singled out? Dwellers of the executive suite are not ordinarily subjected to precognition examinations, brain-dominance surveys, or PSI-Q tests to determine their farsightedness as CEOs. Someday perhaps they will be. Ned Herrmann, founder of the Whole Brain Corporation, believes that his surveys (described in Chapter 7) would be useful in screening out CEO candidates whose brain dominance is "too tilted" for them to be all-around leaders. But as of now it's up to the board of directors to do the screening. That in itself takes intuition. CEOs themselves claim the trickiest task in business today is picking an heir apparent. The wisdom of their choice can take years to confirm, and the impact on the organization may be everlasting.

Choosing the CEO's successor is an impressionistic process. So much of it is unspoken and intuitive. A glance or a nod at a board meeting may carry more weight than words when the choice is being made. So the deciding factors may never be known.

Some psychologists make the distinction between CEOs who are managers and those who are leaders. Managers they describe as "transactional," leaders as "transformational." The former serve mainly as company caretakers, keeping things running smoothly. The latter can do that too. But they also operate as barrier-breakers, striking out across uncharted terrain.

Some corporations today, particularly those undergoing great upheavals, are actively seeking a trustworthy steward to restore stability. Most companies, however, want a visionary at the helm. And even though members of the selection committee might shun the term "intuitive," they actually prefer a leader who is.

What, then, are the attributes of a right-brained boss, the creative leader most corporations are supposedly seeking? Right-brained, that is, in the broadest sense. Not simply right-hemisphere-dominated. But right-thinking—to inspire belief in a bright and exciting future. CEOs who fit this description should ideally be:

Farseeing. Able to look beyond the obvious, while considering many alternatives simultaneously.

Introspective. A trial-and-error thinker with a mind that turns in on itself and doesn't tune out internal stimuli.

Impressionable. Open, trusting, spontaneous, and constantly amazed.

Independent. Accepts the risk of going it alone and being ridiculed.

Decisive. Able to infer overall patterns from scraps of information, therefore capable of solving a problem, setting a course, or taking a leap of faith into the future with insufficient information.

Practical. Realizes that making new ideas work is harder than plucking them out of thin air.

Upbeat. Sure that problems can be solved, and not just for the benefit of the corporation but for society as well.

There is another quality worth mentioning, though it is considered beyond any leader's personal control. Being lucky is important. Patricia Ryan, the managing editor of *People* magazine, whose father was a trainer of racehorses, believes you can spot unlucky leaders. She cites the example of two wealthy horse owners. One had a good ear for what the grooms and exercise boys were saying, and demonstrated a knack for buying future champions. The other owner spent more money but couldn't come up with a winner. "I don't like doing business with people who aren't lucky," Ryan says. "It plagues them their whole career."

There is still one more quality that hardly seems laudatory because it smacks of inconsistency. It might most favorably be called flexibility. Actually, it involves a productive sort of contradictoriness: the ability to be cautiously bold by eliminating all unnecessary hazards while still taking chances; also to be ambiguously clear by defining a goal while allowing a lot of maneuvering room on the way to achieving it.

No one candidate is likely to combine all of these leadership qualities. Headhunters, those alchemists who make gold out of matching intangible human elements, believe that selection committees often feel frustrated because they are searching for a composite: a mythical CEO who combines all the traits of the various candidates being considered. "Often they're looking for the impossible dream," says Russell Reynolds, Jr., chairman of the executive search firm that bears his name.

Although his firm's computerized retrieval system keeps tabs on some twenty-seven thousand executives, Reynolds concedes that the "best CEOs tend to come from within." The inside appointment, he believes, is better understood and less of a shock. "Companies do not respond well to shocks," he adds. "It takes a boat a long time to stop rocking."

Some of the worst succession shocks stem from boards that fail to keep a sufficiently detached eye on management. Assessing and replacing top management, after all, is how directors are expected to serve the shareholders. But all too often even outside directors readily accede to the CEO's choice of an heir apparent instead of relying on their own intuition and judgment.

"You see the wrong guy selected a lot," says J. Peter

Grace, the longest-reigning chief executive of a Fortune 500 company, and one who operates almost entirely on gut feeling. He has worn the W.R. Grace & Company crown since his father suffered a stroke in 1945 and telephoned orders from his sickbed to install his son in his place. Ronald Reagan appointed him head of the President's Private Sector Survey on Cost Control in 1982. And while he now barnstorms the country preaching the gospel of waste-cutting in government, he still clings to his company title.

The blunt-speaking Grace says he would be "appalled" if the board went outside to find his successor. Nevertheless, as CEO, he instinctively prefers to deal with outside directors. "When I first took over, the board was dominated by inside directors," he says. "I found out how dangerous that situation is. Because the chief executive is superior to these people for twenty-nine days a month, you find them sticking it to you on the thirtieth day. Two or three might even close ranks and say, 'We don't like the way he's pushing us around.' "

CAN A BOARD OF DIRECTORS BE INTUITIVE?

Although boards may no longer be limited to the CEO's golfing partners, they are usually dominated by the chairman and two or three other directors. President Reagan's former White House personnel director, E. Pendleton James, currently a New York headhunter who specializes in recruiting directors and chairmen, says: "I'm negative on boards as they're now constituted. They're ossified and incestuous." Many directors, he feels, are not tuned in well enough to respond intuitively to the problems of another company. "Directors stay too long at the fair, and serve on too many boards."

Assuming a board is willing to look outside the company for a CEO, James sees a new tendency to look outside its industry as well. He points to CBS chairman Thomas Wyman, recruited from Jolly Green Giant, and Drew

Lewis, the former secretary of transportation, hired to head Warner Amex Cable Communications. "They came after Lewis because he is a man with great leadership and management skills, not because he was a transportation expert," says James, who considers CEO selection the most important use of intuition in business today.

Lewis is regarded in business as a turn-around expert, and he has helped stem the terrible losses at Warner Amex. "It is the basically insecure CEO who always seeks more information," he says. "Confident leaders trust their intuition." Immediately after taking over as secretary of transportation, he was faced with the air traffic controllers strike. He credits Reagan's intuition with breaking the strike. "The President doesn't need any guidance on that kind of situation," says Lewis. But it was also Lewis's gut feeling to hang tough. As a former cabinet member, Lewis is in great demand as a director. He currently sits on the board of Equitable Life, Campbell Soup, SmithKline Beckman, and MTV Networks.

The men and women who sit on numerous boards do not necessarily subscribe to the notion that they cannot be tuned in to several companies' problems at the same time. They say they acquire a sixth sense that helps them not only in the CEO-selection process, but in all policy-setting decisions. Robert Jensen, chairman of E.F. Hutton LBO Inc., sits on the board of seven major corporations, including Irving Trust, Warneco, Singer, and Tiger International. "Something happens in one boardroom," he says, "then a year later a very similar thing happens in another boardroom. So it's a combination of your intuition and experience that's telling you what to do."

Jensen believes that outside directors have one advantage over the CEO in using intuition. "In the day-to-day operation of a company," he says, "problems come at you rapid-fire, so you're more prone to error. In the boardroom there's more chance for contemplation and checking on your initial instincts."

Nancy Reynolds, president of Wexler, Reynolds, Harrison & Schule Inc., a government affairs consulting firm in the capital, is a director of Sears Roebuck, G.D. Searle, and Viacom. "You get a lot out of board meetings simply through osmosis," she says. "I find I learn a great deal by paying attention to the personalities in a company and what I suspect are their priorities. There's a maturity and calm that you look for in people who run big organizations."

President Matina Horner of Radcliffe sits on a number of foundation and corporate boards, including Twentieth Century Fund, National Science Foundation, Time Inc., Liberty Mutual, and the Federal Reserve Bank of Boston. "There is some pretty impressionistic stuff you come to rely on in selecting CEOs," she says. "Subtleties of judgment, like how they are going to be in managing people." Horner, however, used to think it was wrong to factor in the additional information she picked up by virtue of being a trained psychologist. But she no longer does. "I've come to realize," she says, "if you've gone to school and learned a skill, it's stupid to put it aside."

START-UPS ARE A SPECIAL CASE

One of the most ticklish jobs is picking the right boss for a start-up company. The newly appointed CEO must be steeped in entrepreneurial spirit yet instinctively sense the importance of not stepping on the toes of the creative genius who conceived the product. "The relationship between CEO and creator is a delicate one," admits Terry Opdendyk of ONSET, the Palo Alto seed fund. "The creator is usually the first to suggest that a professional manager be brought in. He knows he needs blockers and tacklers to score. But he doesn't want to lose control of the company's creative direction."

Opdendyk says that he and his partners rely mainly on their own intuition in matching creators and CEOs. The special qualities they look for in the CEO are: (1) general management experience with a track record in growth; (2) great resourcefulness and the ability to operate with a tiny staff; (3) experience in a very entrepreneurial-style company.

"Usually the best choices are not very creative themselves," adds Opdendyk. "The dangerous CEO is one who thinks he's as creative as the entrepreneur. Then you're hiring the guy for the wrong skill-set. It's like hiring an orchestra conductor who thinks he can play the fiddle better than the first violinist."

ONSET's partners believe that the right combination nevertheless produces plenty of creative tension. "The CEO has an equal passion for prestige and money," says Opdendyk. "But his hunger leads him in a different direction. It's all centered on execution."

A CEO WITH KALEIDOSCOPIC VISION

Picking any new CEO involves betting on potential. It's never a sure thing. Giant corporations like General Motors establish a series of steps in the hierarchy so candidates will pop up predictably from within. Some big companies like Citicorp and General Electric create a cadre of equals directly under the CEO to see who seems to have the right stuff for the future. "The surprises in these big companies are how the new CEO will behave," says Rosabeth Moss Kanter, chairman of the Cambridge, Massachusetts, consulting firm Goodmeasure Inc. and sociology professor at the Yale School of Management. "I think it's a big surprise to everyone how intuitively Roger Smith is operating at GM."

Kanter claims that the former chief financial officer "has behaved precisely the way the critics of his appointment claimed he wouldn't be able to." Smith has displayed what Kanter calls "kaleidoscopic thinking"—the ability to see new patterns in old phenomena. "He has taken a set of existing fragments, twisted them, and come up with an exciting new view," she says. But he also had to convey this vision to his colleagues. Shortly after he assumed command, Smith took his nine hundred top executives off on a five-day retreat to pass on his new concepts.

This inward-viewing process that Kanter attributes to Smith is reminiscent of the Zen Buddhist's way of looking at things: peering into the essential nature of a phenomenon until an illuminating new perception (*satori*) suddenly smites the conscious mind. Japanese CEOs might therefore be expected to be especially good at this intuitive grasping of business problems and prospects. Not so, says psychologist Robert Doktor, a University of Hawaii professor who several years ago wired up a number of American CEOs to an electroencephalograph to find out which brain hemisphere they rely on more.

After concluding that American CEOs are action-oriented and essentially right-brain–dominated, Doktor has spent much of the past three years shuttling to Asia to observe some of the biggest bosses in Japan, South Korea, and Hong Kong. "Each one heads a multibillion-dollar corporation," he says. Although he didn't try to use an electroencephalograph, Doktor was permitted to spend a week at the side of each CEO, watching him in action.

"Japanese CEOs are very paced, methodical, and analytic," he says. "They usually spend an hour or so on a single activity before tackling the next and handle only five or six tasks in a day. They are reflective and sensitive to their subordinates. But contrary to myth, they are not very intuitive." South Korean CEOs, Doktor found, model themselves on the Japanese, while the Hong Kong Chinese, mostly Western-educated, copy their American counterparts and jump helter-skelter from task to task.

In Asia or America, or anywhere else for that matter, new products and systems always stir skepticism. So the only time a new venture is tackled is when somebody is willing to take a chance. This means a risk-taker has to be running things. Rosabeth Kanter urges corporations to be more explicit about which parts of the organization should be governed by stable administrative types, and which parts require intuitive entrepreneurial heads. "A different set of tools, techniques, and tactics is required," she says. She calls the intuitive types "change masters," which is the title of her latest book.

But decisions based on gut feelings are hard to explain. As the Zen Buddhists remind us: "Great poetry is born in silence." The Buddhists, however, perceive an inner truth that doesn't easily communicate. The boss, on the other hand, must somehow inspire a sense of collective truth in what he's doing and thereby attract a following. In all intuitive leaps, it's not just the brilliance of the idea that's important but the heat of the enthusiasm that is generated. This need for fire in the boss's belly applies to both start-ups and big corporations. Without it there's no way of winning the people and money needed to put an intuitive idea across.

16

INTUITION'S TRICKLE-DOWN EFFECT

As the men and women interviewed in earlier chapters reveal, running a corporation is a lot more chaotic and less systematic than is generally assumed. Overloaded with work, always under pressure, facing unending interruptions, CEOs are challenged to gain control of their own time and turn obligations into opportunities. The most difficult part of their job is preserving enough time to ruminate on new ways of improving the system—or to use their "golden gut," as psychologist Richard Farson, president of the Western Behavioral Sciences Institute, calls it. "That's why CEOs are paid such high salaries," he maintains.

Improving the system requires leaving room for the Eureka factor to operate. Not just at the top. But all the way down the executive ladder. Several big corporations are beginning to recognize this and are bringing in advisers from such outfits as the Whole Brain Corporation, Inferential Focus, and the National Training Laboratory to demonstrate how to stimulate Mover, or right-brain thinking.

In many companies this creative spirit clashes openly with administrative requirements. Author-consultant Rosabeth Kanter reports that Exxon, one of her clients, is "trying to strike down a lot of rules that inhibit individual judgment" throughout the corporate labyrinth. Procter & Gamble, another client, has started running courses for executives "on how to direct their instincts toward productive results." She also says that Apple, which employs her too, is "making intuition and vision a theme of its leadership."

Kanter realizes that innovators like Xerox's inventor, Chester Carlson, or Apple's cofounder Steven Jobs are inner-directed. They follow their own schedule and feel responsible for their own destiny. Most remarkable is the way they seize on a need for change, while observing the identical problems plaguing their peers. But, adds Kanter, "Intuition is not totally inside the head of the innovator. Part of it comes from being immersed in a business, keeping close to the buyers of a product, and really knowing the field. So by the time a hunch surfaces, it's grounded in reality."

But even the creative Ms. Kanter can't conceal her consultant's stripes when it comes to giving intuition free rein. "I'd be scared of a system in which unbridled intuition runs the corporation," she warns. Yet all the way down the corporate ranks, creativity and autonomy appear increasingly intertwined in the minds of executives. No matter how well they're paid, young managers, especially, no longer want to be on the receiving end of faits accomplis. They want a decision-making role.

Nationwide executive surveys indicate that today autonomy is even more important than pay in determining job satisfaction. Usually those earning higher salaries already enjoy wider freedom. Nevertheless, a deep personal need for achievement is frequently mentioned as an unsatisfied desire. The rewards yearned for seem to come under some vague heading like "psychic income."

LIBERATING THE INNOVATORS

A few farseeing CEOs are effectively cashing in on the innovations such yearning can produce. Lewis W. Lehr, chairman of 3M, had repeatedly stated that its corporate structure is "designed specifically to encourage young entrepreneurs to take an idea and run with it." That approach, he said, "is not a sideline at 3M. It is the heart of our design for growth." John Welch announced when he took over as chairman of GE in 1982 that the giant corporation was going to "act with the agility of a small company."

Gifford Pinchot's book *Intrapreneuring*, expounding on the need to provide entrepreneurial opportunity within big corporations, proved to be an eye-opener to traditional CEOs when it was published in 1985. It describes how small, independent groups of action-takers are working within many corporations to circumvent—even sabotage— the formal systems supposedly managing innovation. The book urges management to underwrite and liberate the real innovators so they don't have to bootleg company resources and steal company time to work on their pet projects.

TAPPING INTO YOUR SUBORDINATES' INTUITION

"It's easy to step in and say I have a feeling we ought to do this or that," says Robert Jensen, chairman of E.F. Hutton LBO. "But then you haven't let your managers weigh in with their feelings first." Several years ago, as chairman and CEO of General Cable Corporation before it was taken over by Penn Central, Jensen found himself facing $300 million in sell-offs and acquisitions. The company had to diversify to survive. "But on each decision," recalls Jensen, "the mathematical analysis only got me to the point where my intuition had to take over. It's not that the numbers weren't accurate. But were the underlying assumptions correct?" To determine if they were, Jensen says, he plumbed the collective intuition of his management team. "This is different," he adds, "than the perfectionist who keeps seeking new advice and never gets anything done."

RELAXING OFFICE ROUTINES

An informal company atmosphere often encourages creativity. Women, who now own 3 million American enterprises and are starting new businesses five times faster than men, have had a lot to do with relaxing office routines. Since many of them are mothers, they are also trying to reduce parental stress by establishing a less hierarchical workplace.

Less hierarchical can also mean more hectic. Debbi Fields, who bore three daughters and built her $30 million-a-year business by the time she was twenty-nine, breathlessly describes the Park City, Utah, headquarters of Mrs. Fields Cookies as "being in a state of perpetual pandemonium. We don't have committees," she says. "I run through the halls talking to people. I gather ideas. I gather other inputs. The doors of my office are never closed. In fact, the size of my office has been cut down three times to make space for new people and it's about to be cut down a fourth time, though it's already teeny-tiny."

But the young and effervescent Mrs. Fields attributes the responsiveness of her two thousand employees to this breakneck pace. "When we decide to do something, we do it," she says. "We are very reactive. We are also very aggressive. There is no such thing as impossible." During the eight years it took her to go from one store in Palo Alto, California, to more than two hundred stores in the United States, Asia, and Australia, she has recited over and over again, both in her mind and aloud: "The one thing I absolutely want to do is make people smile." (Remember the importance of rehearsing an intuitive idea.) She admits, "There's a difficulty trying to make a business out of making people smile." Nevertheless, she says that is her personal statement about "how I feel a business should be run." She wants the employees who work for her, as well as all the customers who come in to buy her cookies, to have an enjoyable experience. "You can't build a business like this simply being logical."

Debbi Fields claims that her husband, Randy, who is executive vice president, supplies all the necessary logic. As head of a financial services firm with assets of $60 million, he also supplied the $50,000 seed money that launched Debbi's business in 1977. "But if Randy had his way," she says, "all our cookies would be made with margarine, and our whole office routine would be just as artificially smooth."

Deborah Szekely, founder of the renowned Golden Door spa in Escondido, California, which has helped slim down so many of America's celebrities, thinks dull office routines are like boring weight-loss regimens. "They burn out their followers before anything constructive is accomplished," she says. "Both," she adds, "must be entered into with a spirit of joy to succeed."

Some male CEOs have similarly established low-protocol, high-spirited workplaces. The Tarkenton Productivity Group is headquartered in Atlanta's Tower Place, an imposing green glass-sheathed skyscraper on Peachtree Road. Yet the dress and atmosphere of the former quarterback's management consulting firm are so casual, and the operatives so laid back, it's hard to tell the chiefs from the Indians. Chairman Fran Tarkenton chews Red Man and drinks Colombian cinnamon decaffeinated coffee from a mug that says "To someone who is outstanding in the field." His office uniform is a sweater, jeans, and running shoes sans socks. "Once," says a colleague, "Fran decided we should all be more professional and wear suits and ties. The edict lasted a day."

Unlike his subordinates, who go through channels in soliciting new clients, Fran goes right to the top—to the Lee Iacoccas, Roger Smiths, and Peter Graces. "The first time I went to see Peter Grace," says Tarkenton, "he was in a meeting. He came out and we talked for half an hour, keeping everybody else waiting. What he really wanted to do was arm wrestle me." Tarkenton declined, fearing that if he won the match he'd lose a client.

Don't be deceived by the informality. Sharon Brown, Tarkenton's secretary, schedules his business trips very tightly, planning a breakfast, lunch, and dinner meeting for every day he's on the road. And his firm has prospered from its relaxed atmosphere, growing to some sixty-five employees and fifty clients.

Continental Airlines chairman Frank Lorenzo's office is a spartan twelve-by-fifteen-foot room in Houston's America

Tower. Once a secluded corporate aerie visited mainly by bankers and lawyers, it is today a common post into which troops everybody, from pilots, flight attendants, and dispatchers to a manufacturer's rep come to peddle a newly designed airplane seat with improved lumbar support. If the traffic gets too heavy upstairs, Lorenzo slips downstairs and goes for a run of six or seven miles on the mulched jogging track that passes right by the building. He is often joined by Continental's number-two man, President Philip Bakes, Jr., who knows that's one time he can catch the boss's undivided attention.

WHIPPING THE COMPANY INTO SHAPE

The business world's biggest exponent of jogging is Joseph McKinney, chairman of the Tyler Corporation. His top team is literally laced into its track shoes a good part of the day, and the company's principal promotion consists of an annual footrace, the Tyler Cup, organized for CEOs over forty years old from all over the United States and Europe.

What has running got to do with creativity and success? "Methinks that the moment my legs begin to move, my thoughts begin to flow," said Henry David Thoreau. McKinney is less poetic and more profit-oriented. "Running, like business, is full of drudgery," he says. "Inherent in our philosophy is the belief that physical fitness gives us a head start over a less fit competitor." The whippetlike appearance of most Tyler executives suggests what McKinney really wants is a spring-legged crew that can run its competitors into the ground. At least that has been the case since Dr. Kenneth Cooper, the father of aerobics, joined the Tyler family.

McKinney encouraged air force heart specialist Cooper, whose books on aerobics have now sold more than 10 million copies, to muster out of the service and build the Aerobics Center in Dallas. (The Tyler Corporation also loaned Cooper $1.25 million to launch the center.) Almost any afternoon now, a covey of sinewy Tyler executives can be seen clip-clopping along its Tartan-surfaced running track, which meanders for a mile through the pecan and persimmon trees. Some of the Tyler Corporation's most fruitful brainstorming occurs après jogging in the sauna and steam rooms.

A combination of the heart, lung, and leg strengthening of aerobics, and the self-image improvement of psychocybernetics, which McKinney had previously learned from Dr. Maxwell Maltz, became his business elixir. He still tries to explain it to other executives out on the banquet circuit with all the fervor of a faith healer. But after a long cocktail hour and full-course dinner, words like "psychocybernetics" and "aerobics" fall on unreceptive ears. What sticks in his listeners' minds, though, is how McKinney has taken Tyler from nowhere to an even 300th on the 1985 Fortune 500 list.

HAIL TO THE FUTURE MBI!

Whether or not they run on a track, most chief executives are strongly oriented to action. Management studies consistently show that they run themselves at an unrelenting pace. The boss's activities are characterized by brevity, variety, and discontinuity. But business leaders are simply reacting to today's tumultous environment. The spastic, patchy, turbulent times in which we now live require all of us to travel more on our instincts. Confidence in analysis has been shaken by the quicksand we are walking across, not by missteps in the logic being applied. If economic uncertainty is, indeed, the father of invention, we can look to a lot more intuitive decision-making and a lot more innovation. What manner of CEO does this portend? The future boss is going to be even more entrepreneurial, a bigger risk-taker, and a more highly intuitive creature than he or she is today.

Psychologists studying the executive animal tell us there's going to be more concern with individuality and creativity all the way down the organization. There's going to be a restoration of the self. Not the narcissistic, self-absorbed one, but the intuitive one that's self-possessed. However, there's a price future leaders will have to pay for granting this freedom—the discomfort caused by their own people going against the grain.

Much of the CEO's discomfort may be self-generated. Psychiatrist Abraham Zaleznik of the Harvard Business School warns that a boss's "ability to see things in new ways requires some flirtation with absurdity and humiliation." He believes that it is the risk of ridicule which also often stifles innovation. "Even farseeing executives with power want to feel comfortable," he says. "Their need for security is not to be underestimated. Yet pursuing an intuitive idea demands that they tolerate painful feelings."

But the fear of being embarrassed by following a gut feeling may not be as bad as the anguish felt from a missed opportunity. We've all heard the lament of leaders who regret not obeying that indescribable sensation in the pit of the stomach: "I should have listened to my gut." Remember "cosmic fishing," Buckminster Fuller's definition of intuition? "Once you feel a nibble," he said, "you've got to hook the fish." Well, a full creel from cosmic fishing requires confidence that you can catch the fish. Not just hook it. But reel it in and land it.

American entrepreneurs have been good fishermen. A worldwide mystique emanates from California's Silicon Valley, Route 128 in Boston, and from our other centers of high-tech creativity. Fortunately we have a business system that tolerates differences and individuality. But innovation still means bucking the trend, even taking a far-out, unpopular stand. That's why trusting your intuition is so important. Remind yourself that the payoff can be enormous. Not just in profits, but in acclaim. Beneficiaries of the Eureka factor are feted as folk heroes here at home and viewed as bright capitalist stars from abroad.

In the future, the higher the rank of the decision-maker, probably the more imperfect will be the data used to make the decision. But then, executives on loftier perches have always been concerned with broader-gauge, longer-term challenges where specific problems are hard to see. Also, those higher-ranking decision-makers have traditionally encountered more opportunities for using nonlogical, intu-

itive approaches in whatever they were doing, whether it
was realizing the mind-blowing applications of Chester
Carlson's xerography or marketing the mouth-watering
appeal of Debbi Fields's cookies.

The intuitive boss who can spot such changes in taste or
technology early on is the kind of leader whose time has
come. Remember the Organization Man, clad in his gray
flannel suit? He thrived in the heyday of smokestack
America, when the corporation was the "citadel of belong-
ingness," as author William H. Whyte, Jr., called it. "Be
loyal to the company and the company will be loyal to you"
went the litany of the fifties. But the Organization Man,
once the idol of an autocratic, regulated industrial era,
succumbed to the free spirit of high technology and the shift
to a service economy. "Upward mobility!" is the cry of our
new meritocracy. Its members boast that their aim of quick
success is as American as Apple computers. But the biggest
winners tomorrow will be those who can summon from
somewhere deep inside themselves glimpses of the economic landscape ahead and intuitive flashes of the business
opportunities that have yet to surface. Hail to the future
MBI—Master of Business Intuition!

AFTERWORD

BACK in 1974 I was operated on for melanoma, statistically a lethal form of cancer. Intuitively I felt that it was possible to summon the power within my own body to defeat the disease. In fact, my self-concocted therapy consisted of writing an article while I was in New York Hospital, explaining this conviction. It was published the next year in the *Atlantic* and then reprinted as a lead article in *Reader's Digest*, titled "The Black Spot." Hundreds of readers wrote from all over the world, and still occasionally do, to say that my story had helped them, just as the writing of it had helped me.

"What causes melanoma?" I had asked the surgeon. "We're not sure," he said. "Some correlation has been observed between the disease and exposure to the sun. Melanin is the pigment cell that makes you tan. When one of the melanocytes goes berserk, melanoma occurs."

So that was it. The black spot on my back was a burned-out fuse. Like the blown fuse in a car, it could make the whole machine die in its tracks. Die? The surgeon didn't say die. And neither did I—ever. As a soldier in World War II, I never believed there was a bullet with my name on it. And later as a combat correspondent in China, Korea, and Vietnam, dying was for the Chinese, Koreans, or Vietnamese. Not for me.

Lying on my bed, watching the sun dance with its mighty solar intensity on the East River, I decided that I could indeed steel my mind against any further incursion of this thing called melanoma. I could do it no matter how my biopsy turned out. I could believe in immunity, depend on it, feel its power. Suddenly I did. I was immune.

Today, eleven years later, as I sit facing my word processor, finishing this book, I am surer than ever that my intuition back then helped to cut out that malignancy as cleanly and incisively as the surgeon's scalpel, which left nothing more than a meandering eighteen-inch-long scar.

Survival, after all, is the most conclusive validation of intuition's power.

Roy Rowan
Byram, Connecticut
November 1, 1985

DR. ROBERT ANTHONY

__**THE ULTIMATE SECRETS OF TOTAL
SELF-CONFIDENCE**__ 0-425-10170-3/$4.50

Join the successful people who have mastered the principles of Total
Self-Confidence. Put all aspects of your life under your control.

__**DR. ROBERT ANTHONY'S MAGIC POWER
OF SUPER PERSUASION**__ 0-425-10981-X/$3.99

Simple, but powerful. Strengthen your art of communication and be a
top achiever!

__**50 GREAT IDEAS THAT CAN CHANGE
YOUR LIFE**__ 0-425-10421-4/$3.95

Fifty concepts designed to make self-evaluation easier than ever.

__**DR. ROBERT ANTHONY'S ADVANCED
FORMULA FOR TOTAL SUCCESS**__

0-425-10804-X/$3.95

Using simple step-by-step methods, turn your dreams into a reality of
total success!

THE THINK BOOKS

In today's fast-paced, mixed-up world, Dr. Robert Anthony's THINK
books offer solutions of hope, encouragement, and cheer. Every book
contains 80 ideas, each on a separate perforated page—so you can easily
tear out the ones you want to tack up or take with you!

__THINK 0-425-08747-6/$3.50

__THINK AGAIN 0-425-09572-X/$2.95

__THINK ON 0-425-11186-5/$2.95

For Visa , MasterCard and American Express orders ($10 minimum) call: 1-800-631-8571

FOR MAIL ORDERS: CHECK BOOK(S). FILL
OUT COUPON. SEND TO:

BERKLEY PUBLISHING GROUP
390 Murray Hill Pkwy., Dept. B
East Rutherford, NJ 07073

NAME_____

ADDRESS _____

CITY_____

STATE_____ZIP_____

PLEASE ALLOW 6 WEEKS FOR DELIVERY.
PRICES ARE SUBJECT TO CHANGE WITHOUT NOTICE.

POSTAGE AND HANDLING:
$1.50 for one book, 50¢ for each ad-
ditional. Do not exceed $4.50.

BOOK TOTAL $ _____

POSTAGE & HANDLING $ _____

APPLICABLE SALES TAX $ _____
(CA, NJ, NY, PA)

TOTAL AMOUNT DUE $ _____

PAYABLE IN US FUNDS.
(No cash orders accepted.)

244